COLUMBIA UNIVERSITY
LIBRARIES

ALASKA PLACE NAMES
THIRD EDITION

Alan Edward Schorr

THE DENALI PRESS

Denali, a Tanaina Indian word meaning " the great one, " is the native name for Mount McKinley. Mount McKinley, at 20,320 feet, the highest mountain on the North American continent, is located in Denali National Park.

Published by The Denali Press
           Post Office Box 1535
           Juneau, Alaska USA 99802-1535

Orders for Alaska Place Names should include payment or purchase order for $15.95 plus $1.50 for shipping.

© The Denali Press

Cover design by John Frailey

All rights reserved. No part of this publication may be reproduced, stored in a retrieval system, or transmitted in any form or by any means, electronic, mechanical, photocopying, recording or otherwise, without the prior written permission of the copyright owner.

All precautions have been made to avoid errors. However, the publishers do not assume and hereby disclaim any liability to any party for any loss or damage caused by errors or omissions, whether said errors or omissions result from negligence, accident or any cause.

LIBRARY CATALOGING DATA

Schorr, Alan Edward
    Alaska Place Names / edited by Alan Edward Schorr. - 3rd
  ed. - [Juneau, Alaska]: The Denali Press [1986]
    144p. ; 28 cm.
    Includes index.
    ISBN 0-938737-11-2
    1. Alaska - Gazetteers. I. Title.
F902.S36   1986   917.98'00321

Printed and bound in the USA

CONTENTS

Preface 7

Alaska Place Names 13

Index 139

PREFACE

Since the publication of Donald Orth's <u>Dictionary of Alaska Place Names</u>[1] in 1967 many new or revised place names have been recognized by the United States Board on Geographic Names (BGN). THe BGN is a federal body charged with providing for uniformity of geographic nomenclature and spelling.[2] To meet the critical need for current place name information for Alaska this writer issued supplements to Orth's monograph in 1974[3] and 1980[4], under the title <u>Alaska Place Names</u>. Due to the continued interest in this subject it was decided to publish a twenty-year cumulation of all decisions on Alaska rendered by

---

[1]Washington, D. C. United States Geological Survey. <u>Professional Paper</u> 567. (reprinted 1971, out of print.)

[2]The antecedents of the BGN can be traced to the late nineteenth century when an informal working group consisting of representatives of the Coast and Geodetic Survey, Geological Survey, Hydrographic Office, Light-House Board, Smithsonian Institution, State, War and Post Office Departments began meeting to solve the problem of supplying accurate and consistent place names for use in preparing maps, charts and other federal publications. In 1890 under the leadership of the Board's first chairman, Professor Thomas C. Mendenhall, the purpose of the Board was to provide for "... uniform usage in regard to geographic nomenclature and orthography ... throughout the Executive Departments of the Government." The basic mission of the Board has not changed in nearly a century.

[3]Issued as No. 2 in the University of Alaska, Fairbanks <u>Elmer E. Rasmuson Library Occasional Papers</u> (out of print).

[4]Issued as No. 1 in the University of Alaska, Juneau <u>Library Occasional Papers</u> (out of print).

the BGN from January, 1966 through December, 1985.[5] Thus, the third edition of <u>Alaska Place Names</u> provides the most up-to-date coverage and includes approximately 1,100 Alaska place names recognized by the Board on Geographic Names.

Included in the third edition of <u>Alaska Place Names</u> are the following categories: 1) new names; 2) new names representing a change in an earlier decision or historical reference; 3) previously established names with revised descriptions and 4) references from previous decisions and variant spellings to the approved name. Names in upper case letters indicate present day usage; names in lower case represent previous decisions and variant spellings.

Generally entries conform to the following format: approved name; geographic designation; elevation or population; description; geographical coordinates; and unapproved previous decision and variant spelling which are listed following the word "Not". Former decisions which are no longer in force are noted as "Vacated".[6]

---

[5] Data originally appeared in the January, 1966 - December, 1985 issues of the BGN <u>Decision List</u> (nos. 6601-8504).

[6] A glossary of terms and a list of abbreviations used in <u>Alaska Place Names</u> may be found in the <u>Dictionary of Alaska Place Names</u>, vi-x and the "Foreward" in issues of the <u>Decision List</u>.

At the end of each approved name is the historical reference or decision date for the name chosen. New names contain reference to the year of the BGN decision. However, new names representing a change in a previous decision, and already established names with revised descriptions, provide reference to both the year of the earlier decision or historical reference as well as to the most recent Board decision.

A new feature of the third edition is an index to personal names, corporate bodies, vessels and other significant information contained in the body of the entry. For the first time these important references can be easily accessed.

Over a century ago Professor John Stuart Blackie, University of Edinburgh, noted that

> . . . it is not only in commemorating special historical events that local names act as an important adjunct to written records; they give likewise the clue to great ethnological facts and movements of which written history preserves no trace. In this respect topographical etymology presents a striking analogy to geology; for, as the science of the constitution of the earth's crust reveals a fossilised history of life in significant succession, long antecedent to the earliest action of the human mind on the objects of terrestrial nature, so the science of language to the practised eye discloses a succession of races in regions where no other sign of their existence remains.[7]

---

[7] C. Blackie. <u>Geographical Etymology: A Dictionary of Place Names</u>. London: Murray, 1887, xxxiii-xxxiv.

Alaska Place Names, to paraphrase a former Executive Secretary of the American Name Society, allows the reader to embark upon a historic and linguistic journey across the frontiers of the Great Land.[8] It is directed to all with an interest in Alaska's past, as well as to those with a special appreciation of its history, geography, or anthropology.

I would like to give sincere thanks to Nancy Fowkes for her generous assistance in the preparation of this manuscript.

Alan Edward Schorr
September, 1986

---

[8]See Illustrated Dictionary of Place Names. New York: Van Nostrand Rheinhold, 1976.

ALASKA PLACE NAMES

ADAMS INLET — estuary, 17.7 km. (11 mi.) long, heads at 58°53'10" N, 135°45'40" W, trends W to Muir Inlet 4.8 km (3 mi.) N of Mount Wright; secs. 10 and 15, T 35 S, R 56 E, Copper River Mer.; 58°50'45" N, 136°03'30" W. BGN 7504.

ADOLPH KNOPF, MOUNT — peak, elevation 1,890 m. (6,200 ft.) in the Coast Mountains 45 km. (28 mi.) NNW of Juneau; named for Adolph Knopf (1882-1966), geologist, U.S. Geological Survey, who did pioneering geologic studies in southeastern Alaska in 1909-1910; secs. 8 and 9, T 37 S, R 64 E, Copper River Mer.; 58°40'45" N, 134°42'07" W. BGN 7602.

AELLO PEAK — peak, elevation 14,445 ft., one of the Twaharpies in the University Range, 4.5 mi. NW of University Peak and 36 mi. ESE of McCarthy; 61°21'55" N, 141°53'55" W. BGN 1967.

AIKEN CREEK — stream, 1.7 mi. long, on Prince of Wales Island, heads in Aiken Lake at 55°06'10" N, 132°13'05" W, flows NNE to Aiken Cove 28 mi. SW of Ketchikan; 55°07'10" N, 132°12'10" W. BGN 1969.

AIKEN LAKE — lake, 1 mi. long, on Prince of Wales Island 29 mi. SW of Ketchikan; 55°06'00" N, 132°13'30" W. BGN 1969.

ALICE, MOUNT — peak, elevation, 1,605 m. (5,265 ft.) in the Kenai Mountains 10 km. (6.2 mi.) NE of Seward; named for Alice Lowell Scheffler, daughter of Captain Frank Lowell who settled in the area in the 1880's; Kenai Peninsula Bor.; sec. 33, T 1 N, R 1 E, Seward Mer.; 60°08'10" N, 149°16'30" W. BGN 8301.

ALINCHAK BAY — bay, 8 km. (5 mi.) wide, on W shore of Shelikof Strait, includes Big Alinchak Bay on the NW and Little Alinchak Bay on the SW, 9.2 km. (5.7 mi.) SW of Mount Kubugakli and 58 km. (36 mi.) NW of Karluk; Tps. 27 and 28 S, Rgs. 36 and 37 W, Seward Mer., 57°47'30" N, 155°16'30" W. BGN 8401.

ALPENGLOW, MOUNT   mountain, elevation over 4,800 ft., on the S side of Turnagain Arm 3.7 mi. SE of the mouth of Sixmile Creek and 12 mi. WNW of Portage; 60°52'32" N, 149°19'55" W. BGN 1969.

ALVERSTONE GLACIER   glacier, 13 mi. long, heads in the Yukon at 60°22' N, 139°06' W, trends S to Hubbard Glacier in the United States, 64 mi. E of Mount Saint Elias; 60°12' N, 139°11' W. BGN 1967.

Amadens Creek   stream, see Kinaruk River.

Amadeus Creek   stream, see Kinaruk River.

AMMUNITION ISLAND   island, 0.32 km. (0.2 mi.) long, most easterly and largest island in the Mineral Creek Islands group, at the far NE end of Port Valdez 2.7 km. (1.7 mi.) NW of Old Valdez, Valdez Bor.; sec. 33, T 8 S, R 6 W, Seward Mer., 61°07'35" N, 146°18'19" W. BGN 8401.

Anangouliak Island   island, see Anangula Island.

Anangula   island, see Anangula island.

ANANGULA ISLAND   island, 2.4 km. (1.5 mi.) long, in the Aleutian Islands off W coast of Umnak Island, 5 km. (3.1 mi.) NNW of Nikolski Bay; 53°00'00" N, 168°54'40" W. Variants: Anaiuliak Island, Anangouliak Island, Anangula, Ananiuliak Island, Ananulyak, Anayulyakh Island, Ostrov Anayulyakh. BGN 7603.

Ananiuliak Island   island, see Anangula Island.

Ananulyak   island, see Anangula Island.

Anayulyakh Island   island, see Anangula Island.

ANDERSON LAKE   lake, 0.97 km. (0.6 mi.) long, separated from Kings Lake on the W by a narrow neck of land, 6.7 km. (4.2 mi.) NE of Wasilla; Matanuska-Susitna Borough, 61°37'15" N, 149°20'00" W; 1978 decision revised. Not: Fishhook Lake, Kings Lake (BGN 1978). BGN 7904.

ANDERSON PEAK	peak, elevation 4,260 ft., S of Ohio Creek, 2 mi. E of Bench Lake and 11 mi. NNE of the village of Moose Pass; named for Paul Anderson, killed July 25, 1968, while working on a project to divert the waters of Ohio Creek; 60°37'02" N, 149°10'22" W. BGN 1969.
ANDESITE POINT	point of land, 0.4 mi., long, elevation over 600 ft., in the Aleutian Islands, on the S coast of Amchitka Island 1 mi. SE of Fumarole Cove; named for its unusually thick layer of andesite lava; 51°32'45" N, 178°54'58" E. BGN 1969.
Andreafski	populated place, see Saint Marys.
Andreafsky	populated place, see Saint Marys.
Andreaoffsky	populated place, see Saint Marys.
ANGAYUKAQSRAQ, MOUNT	mountain, elevation 1,451 mi. (4,760 ft.), in the Baird Mountains 27 km. (17 mi.) SE of Kanaktok Mountain; Eskimo name meaning "old man"; secs. 28, 29, 30, 31, and 32, T 27 N, R 3 W Kateel River Mer.; 67°42'30" N, 159°24'00" W. BGN 7702.
ANGEL, THE	mountain, elevation 9,265 ft., in the Revelation Mountains 12 mi. WNW of Mount Mausolus; 61°41'12" N, 154°11'55" W. BGN 1968.
ANIAKCHAK PEAK	peak, elevation over 4,400 ft., on the S rim of Aniakchak Crater 1.8 mi. SSE of Vent Mountain; 56°51'48" N, 158°07'42" W. BGN 1969.
ANMER CREEK	stream, 3 mi. long, on Snettisham Peninsula, heads at 57°54'10" N, 133°47'03" W, flows NW to Stephens Passage 22 mi. NW of Sumdum; 57°55'28" N, 133°50'00" W. BGN 1969.
ANTLER LAKE	lake, 1.1 mi. long, 10 mi. SE of Lions Head Mountain and 36 mi. NNW of Juneau; 58°46'40" N, 134°50'00" W. BGN 1969.

APOCALYPSE, THE	mountain, elevation 9,345 ft., in Revelation Mountains 10 mi. NW of Mount Mausolus; 61°43'00" N, 154°05'55" W. BGN 1968.
Arcadia Point	point of land, see Westdahl Point.
Archois Peak	mountain, see Arkose Peak.
ARKANSAW CREEK	stream, 4.8 km. (3 mi.) long, heads at 64°05'30" N, 141°00'58" W, flows NW to join Woods Creek to form Canyon Creek 77 km. (48 mi.) S of Eagle; sec. 21, T 27 N, R 22 E, Copper River Mer.; 64°06'40" N, 141°06'40" W. Variants: Brophy Creek, Camp Creek. BGN 7504.
ARKOSE PEAK	mountain, highest elevation over 5,800 ft., at the NE end of Arkose Ridge, 3 mi. SE of Idaho Peak and 13 mi. N of Palmer; 61°47'20" N, 149°03'00" W. Not: Archois Peak. BGN 1969.
ARTILLERY HILL	hill, elevation 580 ft., on Attu Island in the Aleutians Islands, 1 mi. SE of Terrible Mountain and 1 mi. N of Navy Town; 52°51'09" N, 173°11'00" E. BGN 1969.
ASCENSION, MOUNT	mountain, elevation 5,710 ft., in the Kenai Mountains 10 mi. N of Seward; 60°15'33" N, 149°29'45" W. BGN 1969.
ATIGUN GORGE	canyon, 8 mi. long, along the Atigun River 2 mi. E of Galbraith Lake; 68°31'00" N, 149°06'00" W (NE end), 68°27'15" N, 149°21'00" W (SW end). BGN 1972.
ATIGUN PASS	gap, elevation 4,752 ft., in the Endicott Mountains 12 mi. NE of Table Mountain; T 15 S, R 11 E, Umiat Mer., 68°08'00" N, 140°28'15" W. BGN 1972.
Atkasak	village, see Atqasuk.
Atkasook	village, see Atqasuk.
Atkasuk	village, see Atqasuk.

ATQASUK	village, on the W bank of the Meade River 100 km. (62 mi.) ESE of Wainwright and 95 km. (59 mi.) SSW of Barrow; name is an Inupiaq Eskimo work meaning "the place to dig the rock that burns" in reference to a large coal seam located here; North Slope Bor.; sec. 19, T 13 N, R 21 W, Umiat Mer.; 70°28'10" N, 157°23'45" W; 1965 decision revised. Not: Atkasak, Atkasook, Atkasuk, Meade River (BGN 1965), Meade River Village, Mead River, Tikikluk, Tikilook, Tikiluk. BGN 8402.
AVALANCHE SPIRE	peak, elevation 10,105 ft., in the Alaska Range 10 mi. SSW of Mount Hunter; 62°48'25" N, 151°09'00" W. BGN 1968.
Avan Hills	hills, see Avgun Hills.
Avan River	stream, see Avgun River.
AVGUN HILLS	hills, highest elevation 1,405 m. (4,610 ft.), in the De Long Mountains; bound by Kelly River on the W, Kuruk and Kagvik Creeks on the N, Kugururok River on the E, and the flood plain of the Noatak River on the S; bisected by the Avgun River, 128 km. (80 mi.) NNE of Kotzebue; North Slope Bor.; Tps. 31-34 N, Rgs. 12-16 W, Kateel River Mer.; 68°22'00" N, 161°34'30" W (NE end), 68°06'00" N, 162°12'00" W (SW end). Not: Avan Hills. BGN 8503.
AVGUN RIVER	stream, 61 km. (38 mi.) long, heads in the Avgun Hills at 68°18'00" N, 161°50'00" W, flows SW to the Kelly River 9.7 km. (6 mi.) SW of Lake Tagakvik; North Slope Bor.; sec. 9, T 29 N, R 16 W, Kateel River Mer.; 67°55'30" N, 162°20'40" W. Not: Avan River. BGN 8503.

BABEL TOWER	mountain, elevation 8,365 ft., in Revelation Mountains 16 mi. NW of Mount Mausolus; 61°44'24" N, 154°15'20" W. BGN 1968.

BALCHEN, MOUNT	mountain, elevation 3,398 m. (11,140 ft.), in the Alaska Range 7 km. (4.4 mi.) W of Mount Hayes; named for Colonel Bernt Balchen (1899-1973); U.S.A.F., Arctic explorer and aviator; sec. 7, T 15 S, R 5 E, Fairbanks Mer.; 63°37'25" N, 146°50'36" W. BGN 7403.

BALDWIN, MOUNT	mountain, elevation over 8,600 ft., in the Wrangell Mountains, enclosed on the S and W by arms of Hole-in-the-Wall Glacier 10 mi. S of Frederika Mountain; named for George Clyde Baldwin (1884-1951), chief of the U.S. Boundary Survey Parties in Alaska, 1906-1909; secs. 4, 5, 8, and 9, T 3 S, R 18 E, Copper River Mer.; 61°37'38" N, 142°10'15" W. BGN 1970.

BANJO POINT	point of land, in the Aleutian Islands, on the N coast of Amchitka Island 2.3 mi. WNW of Crown Reefer Point; 51°28'43" N, 179°08'13" E. BGN 1969.

BARD PEAK	peak, elevation over 3,800 ft., at the head of Shakespeare Glacier 2.5 mi. SSW of Whittier; 60°44'40" N, 148°43'25" W. Not: Shakespeare Peak, The Cleaver. BGN 1969.

BARREN RIDGE	ridge, 2.2 km. (1.4 mi.) long, in the Terra Cotta Mountains 3.7 km. (2.3 mi.) W of the South Fork Kuskokwim River, 4.5 km. (2.8 mi.) E of the Post River and 37 km. (23 mi.) S of Farewell; 62°12'45" N, 153°29'40" W (NE end), 62°11'50" N, 153°31'20" W (SW end). BGN 8501.

BARRIE ISLAND	island, 0.16 km. (0.1 mi.) long, in Sumner Strait off S coast of Kupreanof Island 1.6 km (1 mi.) SE of Point Barrie; 56°25'35" N, 133°38'00" W. Not: Barrie Islet. BGN 7801.

Barrie Islet	island, see Barrie Island.

BARTLETT HILLS	hills, highest elevation 1,320 ft., 2.5 mi. E. of Talkeetna; named for Edward Lewis (Bob) Bartlett (1904-1968), U.S. Senator from Alaska, 1959 to 1968; 62°20'15" N, 150°00'45" W (N end), 62°16'15" N, 150°00'20" W (S end). BGN 1970.
BARTLETT ISLAND	island, 1.6 km. (1 mi.) long, in Beaufort Sea, 0.8 km. (0.5 mi.) S of Cross Island and 32 km. (20 mi.) NE of Prudhoe Bay; named for Captain Robert Abram Bartlett (1875-1946), master of the <u>Karluk</u>, flagship of the 1913 Stefansson Expedition, which was caught by the ice near this island; North Slope Bor.; 70°28'19" N, 147°57'00" W (N end), 70°27'32" N, 147°56'15" W (S end). Not: No Name Island. BGN 8501.
BASELINE CREEK	stream, 21 km. (13 mi.) long, heads at 69°22'05" N, 145°58'45" W, flows NE to the Kongakut River 24 km. (15 mi.) SSW of Demarcation Point; sec. 24, T 2 N, R 42 E, Umiat Mer.; 69°30'30" N, 141°42'00" W. BGN 7403.
BASKET CREEK	stream, 7 mi. long, on Chichagof Island, heads at 57°36'10" N, 135°02'35" W, flows NE through Basket Lake to Little Basket Bay, 44 mi. NNE of Sitka; 57°38' N, 134°54' W. BGN 1968.
BAT ISLAND	island, 0.2 mi. long, in the Aleutian Islands, along the N coast of Amchitka Island in the W side of Kirilof Bay; named for the triangulation station on the island; 51°25'37" N, 179°14'20" E. BGN 1969.
Battleship Island	island, see Murdo Island.
BAUMANN BUMP	peak, elevation 3,302 ft., on Mount Alyeska 3 mi. ENE of Girdwood; named for Ernst Baumann (1922-1960), who was instrumental in the building of the Alyeska Ski Resort; 60°56'57" N, 149°04'55" W. Not: Max's Mountain. BGN 1970.

BEAR BAY	bay, 1.3 km. (0.8 mi.) wide, on the W shore of Shelikof Strait 6.3 km. (3.9 mi.) SW of Mount Kubugakli and 56 km. (35 mi.) NW of Karluk; T 27 S, R 36 W, Seward Mer.; 57°51'30" N, 155°13'30" W. BGN 8401.
BEAR CREEK	stream,. 27 km. (17 mi.) long, heads at 64°44'30" N, 156°54'20" W, flows N and SW to the Yukon River 12.9 km (8 mi.) NW of Galena; sec 6, T 8 S, R 9 E, Kateel River Mer.; 64°49'08" N, 157°06'35" W. Not: Whakatna Creek. BGN 7704.
Bear Creek	stream, see Whakatna Creek.
BEAUCOUP CREEK	stream, 18.5 km. (11.5 mi.) long, heads in the Philip Smith Mountains at 68°12'00" N, 147°33'25" W, flows SW to the Middle Fork Chandalar River 80 km. (50 mi.) NE of Chandalar; named for the Beaucoup lode copper prospect and claim filed in 1971 on land W of the stream; sec. 20, T 15 S, R 19 E, Umiat Mer.; 68°08'10" N, 147°46'50" W. BGN 7801.
Beercan Lake	lake, see Little Campbell Lake.
BEGICH PEAK	peak, elevation 1,385 m. (4,545 ft.); in the Chugach Mountains 9.7 km. (6 mi.) NW of Whittier; name proposed in 1976 by Senator Ted Stevens to commemorate Alaska Congressman Nicholas Begich (1932-1972), who along with Congressman Thomas Hale Boggs disappeared on October 16, 1972 during an airplane flight from Anchorage to Juneau; sec. 36, T 9 N, R 3 E, and sec. 31, T 9 N, R 4 E, Seward Mer.; 60°49'25" N, 148°49'37: W. BGN 7603.
BELUGA SHOAL	shoal, 7 km. (4.4 mi.) long, in Cook Inlet 43 km. (27 mi.) WSW of Anchorage; named in 1982 by the National Ocean Survey for the Beluga Whales that frequent the area; Kenai Peninsula Bor.; 61°05'11" N, 150°43'30" W (NE end), 61°06'44" N, 150°36'20" W (SW end). BGN 8402.

BEN STEWART, MOUNT	mountain, elevation 1,041 m. (3,415 ft.), 8.9 km. (5.5 mi.) SW of Juneau; named for Benjamin D. Stewart (1878-1976) former mayor of Juneau, Territorial Mine Inspector, and Commissioner of Mines; secs. 35 and 36, T 41 S, R 66 E, Copper River Mer.; 58°16'05" N, 134°33'35" W. BGN 7704.
Bench Glacier	glacier, see Shelf Glacier.
BENCH PEAK	peak, elevation 5,575 ft., 3.8 mi. NE of Bench Lake and 14 mi. SSW of Portage; named for the nearby lake and stream of the same name; SE/4 sec. 32, T 7 N, R 2 E, Seward Mer.; 60°39'00" N, 149°07'55" W. BGN 1971.
BENSON, MOUNT	mountain, elevation 1,304 m. (4,274 ft.), on Kenai Peninsula, in the Kenai Mountains 5 km. (3.1 mi.) NW of Seward; named for Bennie Benson (1913-1972), who designed the Alaska State flag in 1927, while a student in Seward; 60°08'40" N, 149°29'29" W. Variant: Iron Mountain. BGN 7404.
Bernice Lake	populated place, see Port Nikiski.
BIG ALINCHAK BAY	bay, 2.4 km. (1.5 mi.) wide, on the W shore of Shelikof Strait, NW section of Alinchak Bay 12.9 km. (8 mi.) SW of Mount Kubugakli and 58 km. (36 mi.) NW of Karluk; Tps 27 and 28 S, R 37 W, Seward Mer.; 57°48'50" N, 155°18'00" W. BGN 8401.
BIG ALINCHAK CREEK	stream, 10.5 km. (6.5 mi.) long, heads at 57°52'17" N, 155°27'15" W, flows SE to Big Alinchak Bay 14 km. (8.7 mi.) SW of Mount Kubugakli 58 km. (36 mi.) NW of Karluk; sec. 27, T 27 S, R 37 W, Seward Mer.; 57°49'32" N, 155°20'14" W. BGN 8401.
BIG BEAR	creek, Seward Peninsula, tributary to Inglutalik River, near lat. 65°00' N, long. 160°30' W. VACATED. BGN 1910. BGN 1966.

BIG KASHVIK CREEK	stream, 17.9 km. (11.1 mi.) long, heads at 57°59'34" N, 155°20'01" W, flows ESE to Kashvik Bay 6.9 km. (4.3 mi.) NW of Cape Kubugakli and 56 km. (35 mi.) NW of Karluk; sec. 12, T 26 S, R 36 W, Seward Mer.; 57°56'55" N, 155°07'33" W. BGN 8401.
Big Lake	lake, see Bob Johnson Lake.
BIG MERGANSER LAKE	lake, 0.97 km. (0.6 mi.) long, on the Kenai Peninsula 21.7 km (13.5 mi.) NNE of Sterling; named about 1963 by officials of the Kenai National Moose Range, probably for the American Merganser or Pond Shelldrake (Mergus americanus), a large freshwater duck which breeds in southern Alaska; Kenai Peninsula Borough; secs. 2 and 3, T 7 N, R 8 W, Seward Mer.; 60°43'34" N, 150°38'27" W. BGN 8504.
BIG RAM LAKE	lake, 1 mi. long, 5 mi. W of Keche Mountain and 63 mi. NW of Christian; 67°58'45" N, 146°57'20" W. BGN 1971.
BILL BESSER LAKE	lake, 0.97 km. (0.6 mi.) long and 0.32 km. (0.2 mi.) wide, on the Kenai Peninsula, 2.9 km. (1.8 mi.) SSW of Moose Point and 50 km. (31 mi.) NE of Kenai; named for William Besser (1877-1968), Alaska pioneer who lived in Alaska from 1914 to 1956; he owned property on Cook Inlet N of this lake from 1924 to 1955; Kenai Peninsula Bor.; sec. 28, T 10 N, R 8 W, Seward Mer.; 60°55'35" N, 150°42'10" W. BGN 8403.
BILLY MITCHELL, MOUNT	mountain, elevation 7,217 ft., in the Chugach Mountains 12 mi. W of the Copper River and 35 mi. E of Valdez; named for Brigadier General William Mitchell (1879-1936), who, as a lieutenant, was instrumental in constructing a telegraph line from Eagle to Valdez from 1901 to 1902; 61°12'13" N, 145°16'26" W. BGN 1968.

BILLY'S HOLE	lake, 0.6 mi. long and 0.3 mi. wide, along the W coast of Long Bay 1 mi. WNW of Schrader Island; sec. 10, T 10 N, R 12 E, Seward Mer.; 60°58'15" N, 147°17'50" W. BGN 1897. BGN 1972.
Binnyanaktuk Creek	stream, see Pinnyanatuk Creek.
Bird Island	island, see Gull Island.
BITTERSWEET ROCK	rock, in Behm Canal off E coast of Cleveland Peninsula 1.4 km. (0.9 mi.) E of Bond Bay; named for the Coast Guard Cutter *Bittersweet*, which ran aground on this rock searching for a distressed vessel on April 13, 1968; 58°31'45" N, 131°55'40" W. BGN 7501.
BLACK SAND BEACH	beach, 0.24 km. (0.15 mi.) across, on SE coast of Gravina Island 6.4 km. (4 mi.) S of Ketchikan; named for the dark color of the sand; sec. 18, T 76 S, R 91 E, Copper River Mer.; 55°17'10" N, 131°38'05" W. BGN 7704.
BLACK SAND COVE	cove, 0.48 km. (0.3 mi.) across, on SE coast of Gravina Island 6.4 km. (4 mi.) S of Ketchikan; sec. 18, T 76 S, R 91 E, Copper River Mer.; 55°17'10" N, 131°37'40: W. BGN 7704.
Black Warrior Peak	peak, see Silvertip, Mount.
BLACKBURN HILLS	hills, 32 km. (20 mi.) long and 17.7 km. (11 mi.) wide, W of the Yukon River and 58 km. (36 mi.) SE of Unalakleet; 63°31'00" N, 159°50'00" W (N end), 63°15'00" N, 160°01'20" W (S end). BGN 8501.
BLANKENSHIP CREEK	stream, 12 mi. long, heads at 68°36'25" N, 156°45'45" W, flows N to the Ipnavik River 5 mi. WNW of Smith Mountain Lakes; named for Walter R. Blankenship, who was a field hand for USGS northern Alaska field parties from 1924-1926; 68°46'15" N,, 156°37'30" W. BGN 1972.
BLIND LUCK LAKE	lake, 0.97 km. (0.6 mi.) long, 58 km. (36 mi.) SW of Manley Hot Springs; sec. 8 and 17, T 4 S, R 19 W, Fairbanks Mer.; 64°34'40" N, 151°24'20" W. BGN 7504.

Blue Mountain — mountain, see Whale Mountain.

BLUFF GULCH — ravine, 1 mi. long, heads at 67°26'18" N, 150°01'36" W, trends NW to the Middle Fork Koyukuk River 3 mi. NNE of Wiseman; sec. 5, T 30 N, R 11 W, Fairbanks Mer.: 67°26'50" N, 150°03'12" W. BGN 7303.

Bluff Gulch — ravine, see Coon Gulch.

BOAT LAKE — lake, 1.3 km. (0.8 mi.) across, 7.2 km. (4.5 mi.) NNW of Willow Lake and 14.5 km. (9 mi.) NE of Huslia; secs. 11 and 14, T 4 N, R 13 E, Kateel River Mer.; 65°45'20" N, 156°06'00" W. BGN 8202.

Boat Lake — lake, see Willow Lake.

BOB JOHNSON LAKE — lake, 8.1 km. (5 mi.) long, 35 km. (22 mi.) W. of Chandalar, named for Robert R. Johnson (1919-1974), a well-known Alaskan pilot and chief pilot for the Alaska District of the Department of the Interior's Office of Air Service; T 31 N, Rgs. 8 and 9, Fairbanks Mer.; 67°30'00" N, 149°24'00" W. Variant: Big Lake. BGN 7702.

BOCHAROV ISLAND — island, 0.16 km. (0.1 mi.) across, in Constantine Harbor off Hinchinbrook Island 1.1 km. (0.7 mi.) NW of Phipps Point and 53 km. (33 mi.) SW of Cordova; named for Dmitrii Ivanovich Bocharov who as co-commander with G. A. Izmaylov (Izmailov) of the Russian vessel *Three Saints*, buried a metal plate inscribed "Russian Territory, No. 8" on this island in 1788; sec. 33, T 17 S, R 8 W, Copper River Mer.; 60°21'25" N, 146°37'20" W. BGN 7903.

BODENBURG CREEK — stream, 8.4 km. (5.2 mi.) long, heads at 61°34'22" N, 149°01'15" W, flows S to Knik River 11.3 km. (7 mi.) SSE of Palmer; Matanuska-Susitna Borough; sec. 1, T 16 N, R 2 E, Seward Mer.; 61°30'35" N, 149°01'43" W. Not: Palmer Creek. BGN 7902.

BOGGS PEAK   peak, elevation 1,353 m. (4,440 ft.), in the Chugach Mountains 9.7 km. (6 mi.) NW of Whittier; name proposed in 1976 by Senator Ted Stevens to commemorate Louisiana Congressman Thomas Hale Boggs (1914-1972), who disappeared along with Nicholas Begich on October 16, 1972 during an airplane flight from Anchorage to Juneau; sec. 30, T 9 N, R 4 E, Seward Mer.; 60°50'17" N, 148°48'20" W. BGN 7603.

BONANZA CREEK   stream, 1.6 km. (1 mi.) long, on the Kenai Peninsula, heads at 60°49'15" N, 149°30'32" W, flows NW to Palmer Creek 12.1 km. (7.5 mi.) SE of Hope and 77 km. (48 mi.) NNW of Seward; Kenai Peninsula Borough; sec. 36, T 9 N, R 2 W, Seward Mer.; 60°50'00" N, 149°32'08" W. BGN 8002.

BOULDER CREEK   stream, 22 mi. long, heads at 65°10'05" N, 150°47'50" W, flows WSW to Fish Lake 21 mi. SE of Tanana; 65°04'35" N, 151°22'45" W. Not: Fish Creek, Guthna Creek. 1911. BGN 1968.

BOULDER PATCH   area (submerged boulders), 29 km. (18 mi.) long and 10 km. (6.2 mi.) wide, in Stefansson Sound, extends NW from Foggy Island Bay to Cross Island between the McClure Islands and Dinkum Sands on the NE and Point Brower and the Sagavanirktok River Delta on the SW 19.3 km. (12 mi.) E of Prudhoe Bay; named in 1979 by marine geologists of the U.S. Geological Survey; 70°28'00" N, 147°58'00" W (NW end), 70°17'00" N, 147°28'00" W (SE end). BGN 8002.

Boundary Peak 94   peak, see Gisel Peak.

Boundary Peak 100   peak, see London, Mount.

Boundary Peak 101   peak, see Service, Mount.

Boundary Peak 103   peak, see Hislop, Mount.

Boundary Peak 104   peak, see Pullen, Mount.

BOURBON MIST ISLAND   island, 0.15 mi. long, in Whiskey Lake 7.5 mi. WNW of Skwentna and 65 mi. N of Tyonek; 61°59'20" N, 151°23'53" W. BGN 1967.

BOX ISLAND	island, in the Gulf of Alaska off SE coast of Montague Island 0.8 km. (0.5 mi.) ESE of Box Point; 59°57'45" N, 147°20'25" W. BGN 7803.
BRACKETT, MOUNT	peak, elevation 2,225 m. (7,300 ft.), in the Coast Mountains 6.1 km. (3.8 mi.) S of Mount Leland and 51 km. (32 mi.) SE of Skagway; named for George Brackett, who in 1897 constructed a toll road near Skagway during the gold rush; 59°06'57" N, 134°47'45" W. BGN 7904.
BRADLEY LAKE	reservoir, on Kenai Peninsula, formed by damming the Bradley River 5 mi. above its mouth at Kackemak Bay; 59°45'25" N, 150°51'00" W. BGN 1972.
BRADLEY PEAK	peak, elevation 917 m. (3,007 ft.), 2.7 km. (1.7 mi.) SE of Sunrise; named for Lois I. Bradley (died 1974), homesteader who came to Alaska in 1953; sec. 12, T 9 N, R 1 W, Seward Mer.; 60°52'54" N, 149°22'21" W. BGN 7503.
BRAIDED CREEK	stream, 3 mi. long, on Montague Island, heads at 59°55'20" N, 147°36'40" W, flows ESE to the Nellie Martin River 2 mi. W of Patton Bay; 59°54'25" N, 147°32'40" W. BGN 1967.
BREEZY BAY	bay, 4 km. (2.5 mi.) across, in Tlevak Strait on the E coast of Dall Island between Eolus and Boreas Points, 16.1 km (10 mi.) SW of Hydaburg; descriptive name given in 1881 by Lt. Comdr. H. E. Nichols, USN, "on account of the strong winds encountered there"; Tps. 77 and 78 S, R 81 E, Copper River Mer.; 55°09'15" N, 133°03'00" W. BGN 8104.
BRIDAL VEIL FALLS	rapids, 0.8 km. (0.5 mi.) long, in the lower course of Captain William Moore Creek and extending up an unnamed western tributary, 14.2 km. (8.8 mi.) NE of Skagway; 59°34'10" N, 135°12'30" W (NW end), 59°33'55" N, 135°11'25" W (SE end). BGN 8501.

BRIDGE CREEK — stream, 1.5 mi. long, in the Aleutian Islands, heads at 51°26'42" N, 179°09'43" E, flows ENE to Cyril Cove on the N coast of Amchitka Island; named for the bridge crossing this stream, which is the only bridge along Infantry Road; 51°27'06" N, 179°11'26" E. BGN 1969.

BROCK, MOUNT — mountain, elevation 4,990 ft., between Muir and Riggs Glaciers, in the Glacier Bay National Monument, 3 mi. NW of Muir Inlet; named for R. W. Brock, Canadian geologist, who visited Muir Inlet in 1913; 59°06'30" N, 136°15'30" W. Not: Mount Brack. BGN 1967.

BROPHY CREEK — stream, 1.6 km. (1 mi.) long, heads at 64°05'27" N, 141°04'35" W, flows WNW to Camp Creek 3.2 km. (2 mi.) N of Boundary; sec. 28, T 27 N, R 22 E, Copper River Mer.; 64°05'45" N, 141°06'27" W. BGN 7504.

Brophy Creek — stream, see Arkansas Creek.

BROWN BEAR HEAD ISLAND — island, 61 m. (200 ft.) long, in Keku Strait 305 m. (1,000 ft.) S of Beck Island and 50 km. (31 mi.) SW of Petersburg; name derived from a reported incident in which a young Indian man was killed by a brown bear, and later, when the bear was killed, its head was impaled on a pole on the island; sec. 23, T 60 S, R 74 E, Copper River Mer.; 56°39'22" N, 133°42'56" W. BGN 7704.

BUCHIA RIDGE — ridge, 16.1 km. (10 mi.) long, between the Kulukak and Ungalikthluk Rivers 27 km. (17 mi.) ENE of Togiak; named for the abundant fossil shells (Buchia crassicolis) which occur in the rocks along the crest of this ridge; 59°13'00" N, 159°43'00" W (NE end), 59°06'00" N, 159°52'00" W (SW end). BGN 7504.

BUCK VALLEY — valley, 4 km. (2.5 mi.) long, heads at 55°43'30" N, 160°54'45" W, trends ENE to Herendeen Bay 4.8 km. (3 mi.) WNW of Pinnacle Peak and 8.9 km. (5.5 mi.) WSW of the village of Herendeen Bay; T 51 S, R 74 W, Seward Mer.; 55°44'45" N, 160°49'00" W. BGN 8402.

BUDDY CREEK   stream, 11.3 km. (7 mi.) long, heads at 62°09'05" N, 149°50'22" W, flows WSW to Montana Creek 19.3 km. (12 mi.) S of Talkeetna; sec. 33, T 24 N, R 4 W, Seward Mer.; 62°08'00" N, 150°00'53" W. BGN 8301.

BUFFALO DOME   hill, elevation 676 m. (2,218 ft.), 2.4 km. (1.5 mi.) W of the Delta River and 6.4 km. (4 mi.) NW of Donnelly; bison have summered here since they were introduced in the area in the 1920s; secs. 9, 10, 11, 14, 15, and 16, T 14 S, R 9 E, Fairbanks Mer.; 63°42'45" N, 145°58'52" W. BGN 8402.

BUOY POINT   point of land, in the Aleutian Islands, on the S coast of Amchitka Island 1 mi. SW of White House Cove and 1.2 mi. SE of Sandy Cove; named for a buoy found at this place; 51°33'53" N, 178°51'15" E. BGN 1969.

BUTTERFLY LAKE   lake, 1.9 km. (1.2 mi.) long, 43 km. (27 mi.) NW of Anchorage; Matanuska-Susitna Borough; secs. 1, 2, 3, 10, and 11, T 17 N, R 5 W, Seward Mer.; 61°35'30" N, 150°07'45" W; 1968 decision revised. Not: Delyndia Lake, East Butterfly Lake (BGN 1968), West Butterfly Lake (BGN 1968). BGN 7902.

Butterfly Lake   lake, see East Butterfly Lake.

Butterfly Lake   lake, see West Butterfly Lake.

BYRON PEAK   mountain, highest elevation 4,750 ft., at the head of Byron Glacier 7 mi. SW of Whittier; 60°43'42" N, 148°51'55" W. BGN 1969.

C. P. BLUFF	bluff, elevation 610 ft., in the Aleutian Islands, on the NW end of Amchitka Island 1.5 mi. SE of Aleut Point; named for the U.S. AEC Control Point complex erected on the bluff; 51°37'50" N, 178°39'22" E. BGN 1969.
CALLIOPE MOUNTAIN	mountain, elevation 6,810 ft., 2.7 mi. SE of Eagle Lake and 20 mi. ESE of Anchorage; 61°08'34" N, 149°18'35" W. Not: Icy Peak. BGN 1969.
CALLISTO PEAK	peak, elevation 3,657 ft., in the Kenai Mountains 8 mi. S of Seward; 59°59'23" N, 149°29'00" W. BGN 1969.
CAMP CREEK	stream, 3.2 km. (2 mi.) long, heads at 64°04'50" N, 141°04'35" W, flows NW to Woods Creek 3.5 km. (2.2 mi.) N of Boundary; sec. 29, T 27 N, R 22 E, Copper River Mer.; 64°05'55" N, 141°07'00" W. BGN 7504.
Camp Creek	stream, see Arkansaw Creek.
CAMPBELL LAKE	reservoir, 2.1 km. (1.3 mi.) long, along Campbell Creek 8 km. (5 mi.) SSW of Anchorage; secs. 14 and 15, T 12 N, R 4 W, Seward Mer.; 61°08'05" N, 149°56'15" W. BGN 8002.
Campbell Lake	lake, see Little Campbell Lake.
CANNERY POINT	point of land, at the mouth of Port Frederick on the NE coast of Chichagof Island 2.7 km. (1.7 mi.) NW of Hoonah; Sitka Bor.; sec. 20, T 43 S, R 61 E, Copper River Mer.; 58°07'54" N, 135°27'43" W. Not: Inner Point Sophia. BGN 8501.
CANTATA PEAK	peak, elevation 6,410 ft., in Chugach Mountains 20 mi. E of Anchorage; 61°09'30" N, 149°19'10" W. BGN 1968.
CAPEL POINT	point of land, on Wrangell Island on the W shore of Blake Channel 110 km. (68 mi.) NNW of Ketchikan; sec. 16, T 64 S, R 86 E, Copper River Mer.; 56°19'00" N, 131°59'55" W. BGN 8002.

CAPTAIN WILLIAM MOORE CREEK   stream, 9.7 km. (6 mi.) long, heads in
                                      Canada at 59°38'00" N, 135°09'45" W,
                                      flows S into Alaska to Skagway River 3.2
                                      km. (2 mi.) E of Mount Carmack; named
                                      for William Moore, who homesteaded in
                                      1887 on land that is now within the city
                                      of Skagway, Alaska and British Columbia;
                                      sec. 3, T 27 S, R 60 E, Copper River
                                      Mer.; 59°33'45" N, 135°11'27" W.
                                      Variant: Moores Creek. BGN 7402.

CARIBOU ISLAND   island, 1.3 km. (0.8 mi.) long, in
                                      Skilak Lake on the Kenai Peninsula 48
                                      km. (30 mi.) ESE of Kenai; Kenai
                                      Peninsula Borough; secs. 23, 24, 25 26,
                                      T 4 N, R 7 W, Seward Mer.; 60°24'53" N,
                                      150°25'11" W. BGN 8504.

CARLSEN POINT   point of land, on Kodiak Island, on E
                                      side of Uyak Bay at S entrance to Zacher
                                      Bay 9.7 km. (6 mi.) NE of the community
                                      of Larsen Bay; Kodiak Island Borough;
                                      sec. 18, T 30 S, R 28 W, Seward Mer.;
                                      57°34'32" N, 153°50'35" W. BGN 8402.

CARPENTER LAKE   lake, 1 mi. long, 9 mi. WSW of Knik and
                                      15 mi. NNW of Anchorage; secs. 32 and
                                      33, T 16 N, R 4 W, Seward Mer.;
                                      61°26'05" N, 150°01'30" W. BGN 1971.

CASCADE CREEK   stream, 11.3 km. (7 mi.) long, heads at
                                      63°38'18" N, 160°43'55" W, flows NW to
                                      Point Creek E of Norton Sound and 21.2
                                      km. (13.2 mi.) SSW of Unalakleet; sec.
                                      7, T 21 S, R 11 W, Kateel River Mer.;
                                      63°41'25" N, 160°51'53" W. BGN 8103.

Cascade Creek   stream, see Jesse Creek.

CAT SHOALS   shoals, 11.3 km. (7 mi.) long, in the
                                      Beaufort Sea 11.3 km. (7 mi.) NE of the
                                      Jones Islands; so named because depth
                                      contours give the appearance of a
                                      running cat; North Slope Borough,
                                      70°37'42" N, 149°09'42" W (NW end),
                                      70°35'00" N, 148°52'48" W (SE end). BGN
                                      7902.

CAVIAR CREEK   stream, 7 mi. long, on Seward
                                Peninsula, heads in a lake at 65°20'05"
                                N, 163°07'00" W, flows NNE to Koyuk
                                River, 3 mi. NE of Sturgeon Ridge and 13
                                mi. SSE of Imuruk Lake; 65°24'50" N,
                                163°01'10" W. BGN 1952. BGN 1967.

CECIL RHODE MOUNTAIN   peak, elevation 1,343 m. (4,405 ft.),
                                2.7 km. (1.7 mi.) S of Cooper Landing
                                and 4.8 km. (3 mi.) W of Kenai Lake;
                                named for Cecil Rhode (1902-1979),
                                conservationlist and photographer who
                                lived in Cooper Landing for over forty
                                years; Kenai Peninsula Borough; sec. 4,
                                T 4 N, R 3 W, Seward Mer.; 60°28'00" N,
                                149°49'00" W. BGN 8103.

Celenie Lake   cove, see Johnson Slough.

CELENO PEAK   peak, elevation over 13,300 ft., one of
                                the Twaharpies in the University Range,
                                6.5 mi. WNW of University Peak and 34
                                mi. ESE of McCarthy; 61°20'20" N,
                                141°58'10" W. BGN 1967.

CHANDALAR SHELF   plain, 1 mi. long, 0.5 mi. E of the
                                Dietrich River and 5 mi. N of Table
                                Mountain; T 16 S, R 11 E, Umiat Mer.;
                                68°02'45" N, 149°36'45" W. BGN 1969.

CHAPIN PEAK   peak, elevation 2,730 ft., on Gravina
                                Island 12 mi. SW of Ketchikan; named for
                                Theodore S. Chapin (1876-1964), who from
                                1915 to 1917 mapped the geology of
                                Gravina Island while employed as a
                                geologist with the U.S. Geological
                                Survey; 55°12'00" N, 131°47'30" W. BGN
                                1970.

Chefarnok   village, see Chefornak.

CHEFORNAK   village, on the left bank of the Kinia
                                River 9 km. (5.5 mi.) N of Tern
                                Mountain; sec. 20, T 1 N, R 86 W, Seward
                                Mer.; 60°09'35" N, 164°15'55" W.
                                Variants: Chefarnok, Chifornak. BGN
                                7501.

CHELLE LAKE   lake, 2.4 km. (1.5 mi.) long, on NW
                                    slope of Mount Drum 29 km. (18 mi.) SE
                                    of Gulkana; named for Chelle Holen
                                    (1961-1969) daughter of Lee Holen, a
                                    former owner of a lodge on the lake;
                                    secs. 21 and 28, T 5 N, R 3 E, Copper
                                    River Mer.; 62°11'30" N, 144°52'00" W.
                                    BGN 7501.

Chena River   stream, see Middle Fork.

CHEVAL NARROWS   water passage, 2.4 km. (1.5 mi.) long
                                    between Cheval Island and the Aialik
                                    Peninsula on the Kenai Peninsula, 16.9
                                    km. (10.5 mi.) SW of Cape Resurrection;
                                    Kenai Peninsula Borough; T 4 S, R 2 W
                                    and T 5 S, R 2 W, Seward Mer.; 59°46'15"
                                    N, 149°31'30" W. BGN 8003.

Chifornak   village, see Chefornak.

CHIGMIT MOUNTAINS   mountains, 200 km. (125 mi.) long, in
                                    the Aleutian Range, bounded on NW by
                                    Blockade Glacier and Lake, Summit Lake,
                                    Tlikakila River, Lake Clark, Sixmile
                                    Lake, and Newhalen River, on the SW by
                                    Iliamna Lake and on the SE by Cook
                                    Inlet; 61°00'00" N, 152°08'00" W (NE
                                    end), 59°25'00" N, 154°20'00" W (SW
                                    end). Variant: Tschigmit Gebirge. BGN
                                    7603.

Chigmit Mountains   mountains, see Neacola Mountains.

CHIGNAKI POND   lake, 0.48 km. (0.3 mi.) across, 5.6
                                    km. (3.5 mi.) NW of Wasilla;
                                    Matanuska-Susitna Borough; secs. 20 and
                                    29, T 18 N, R 1 W, Seward Mer.;
                                    61°37'40" N, 149°29'05" W. BGN 8002.

CHIJUK CREEK   stream, 43 km. (27 mi.) long, heads 2.4
                                    km. (1.5 mi.) NE of Schnieder Lake at
                                    62°11'22" N, 150°39'10" W, flows SSE to
                                    Kroto Creek 24.1 km. (15 mi.) NW of
                                    Willow; named for a former headman of
                                    the Nulchina clan residing in the Kroto
                                    area who died in the 1930's;
                                    Matanuska-Susitna Borough; sec. 28, T 21
                                    N, R 6 W, Seward Mer.; 61°53'00" N,
                                    150°23'45" W. BGN 8502.

CHINA POOT LAKE	lake, 1.3 mi. long, on Kenai Peninsula, 0.8 mi. E. of China Poot Bay and 13 mi. SE of Homer; 59°32'30" N, 151°12'30" W. BGN 1967.
CHINEEKLUK LAKE	lake, 0.64 (0.4 mi.) long, in the upper course of Chineekluk Creek, on the N slope of the Chuilnuk Mountains 48 km. (30 mi.) SW of Sleetmute; sec. 3, T 14 N, R 48 W, Seward Mer.; 61°20'15" N, 157°52'25" W. BGN 8301.
CHINOOK CREEK	stream, 16.1 km. (10 mi.) long, in the Talkeetna Mountains, heads at 62°42'25" N, 149°11'30" W, flows N to the Susitna River 27 km. (17 mi.) ENE of the community of Gold Creek; named for the chinook salmon which were first spotted in the stream in 1982; Matanuska-Susitna Bor.; sec. 6, T 31 N, R 2 E, Seward Mer.; 62°48'09" N, 149°09'47" W. BGN 8403.
CHITKA RIDGE	ridge, 1.2 mi. long, elevation 1,100 ft., in the Aleutian Islands, on Amchitka Island just W of Chitka Cove; named for the cove; 51°36'18" N, 178°54'45" E (NE end), 51°35'35" N, 178°53'40" E (SW end). BGN 1969.
CHUATHBALUK	settlement, on the N bank of the Kuskokwim River 9.5 mi. E of Aniak; 61°34'15" N, 159°14'40" W. Not: Little Russina Mission, Lower Russian Mission, Russian Mission (former decision). BGN 1948. BGN 1969.
CHURCH, MOUNT	peak, elevation 2,509 m. (8,233 ft.), in Denali National Park and Preserve, on the SE slope of Mount McKinley 8 km. (5 mi.) S of Mount Dickey; sec. 12, T 32 N, R 8 W, Seward Mer.; 62°52'45" N, 150°41'00" W. Not: Mount Genet. BGN 8501.
CLAM POINT	point of land, in the Aleutian islands, on the S coast of Amchitka Island 0.8 mi. NNW of Rifle Range Point; named for the fossil clams found in the rocks; 51°24'34" N, 179°09'43" E. BGN 1969.

CLARENCE KRAMER PEAK	peak, elevation 1,280 m. (4,200 ft.), on an unnamed mountain 1.5 km. (0.9 mi.) N of Blue Lake and 10.8 km. (6.7 mi.) ENE of Sitka on Baranof Island; named for Clarence E. Kramer (?-1978), logger and civic leader who held important positions in lumbering associations and who was named "Outstanding Alaskan" by the State Chamber of Commerce in 1977; sec. 24, T 55 S, R 64 W, Copper River Mer., 57°05'30" N, 135°10'00" W. BGN 7902.
CLAY LAKE	lake, 0.97 km. (0.6 mi.) long, along the course of Marten Creek 27 km. (17 mi.) SSE of Nelson Glacier and 102 km. (63 mi.) NNW of Ketchikan; secs. 6 and 7, T 65 S, R 88 E, Copper River Mer.; 56°15'25" N, 131°51'40" W; 1978 description revised. BGN 8002.
Cleaver, The	peak, see Bard Peak.
COAL MINE CREEK	stream, 6.6 km. (4.1 mi.) long, heads at 63°41'28" N, 160°43'00" W, flows NW to Norton Sound between Jesse and Glacier Creeks 16.9 km. (10.5 mi.) S of Unalakleet; sec. 33, T 20 S, R 11 W, Kateel River, Mer.; 63°43'10" N, 160°49'20" W. Not: Glacier Creek. BGN 8103.
Coal Mine Creek	stream, see Summer Camp Creek.
COLUMN RIDGE	ridge, 1.5 mi. long in the Aleutian islands, on the S side of Amchitka Island 0.8 mi. E of Signal Cove and 7.5 mi. SE of Aleut Point; named for the thick lava flows that display well-developed vertical columns as much as 200 ft. high; 51°34'40" N, 178°46'40" E (SW end), 51°35'45" N, 178°47'35" E (NE end). BGN 1969.
COLUMN ROCKS	rocks, on the Aleutian Islands, off the S coast of Amchitka Island 2 mi. SW of Buoy Point and 2.3 mi. SE of Windy Island; named for the well-developed columnar jointing; 51°32'27" N, 178°49'25" E. BGN 1969.

CONCLUSION CREEK	stream, 2.2 mi. long, on Baranof Island, heads at 56°14'47" N, 134°43'50" W, flows E to Port Conclusion 1.5 mi. W of Port Alexander; 56°14'50" N, 134°41'00" W. BGN 1969.
CONFUSION POINT	point of land, in Johns Hopkins Inlet 6 mi. W of Russell Island; 58°54'10" N, 136°59'25" W. BGN 1972.
Cool Sac Glacier	glacier, see Cul-de-sac Glacier.
COON GULCH	ravine, 2.3 mi. long, heads at 67°26'43" N, 149°58'54" W, trends N to the Middle Fork Koyukuk River valley 4.5 mi. NE of Wiseman; sec. 4, T 30 N, R 11 W, Fairbanks Mer.; 67°27'40" N, 150°01'12" W. Variant: Bluff Gulch. BGN 7303.
COOPER, MOUNT	mountain, elevation 2,067 m. (6,780 ft.) in the Saint Elias Mountains, at the head of Kashoto Glacier, 4 km. (2.5 mi.) S of Johns Hopkins Inlet, and 97 km. (60 mi.) SW of Haines; named for Dr. William Skinner Cooper (1884-1978), plant ecologist who performed several vegetation-glacier relationship studies in the Glacier Bay area and was chairman of the committee of scientists which initiated the proposal to establish Glacier Bay National Monument; sec. 6, T 35 S, R 51 E, Copper River Mer.; 58°51'45" N, 136°58'53" W. BGN 8001.
Copper City	populated place, see Valdez.
CORNER CREEK	stream, 6 mi. long, on Chichagof Island, heads at 57°41'35" N, 135°07'02" W, flows SSE 1 mi., then N, to Corner Bay 48 mi. NNE of Sitka; 57°43'45" N, 135°07'00" W. BGN 1968.
COXCOMB POINT	point of land, on Kenai Peninsula, at the entrance to Kings Bay from Port Nellie Juan 2.4 km. (1.5 mi.) NW of Greystone Bay; secs. 7 and 8, T 5 N, R 6 E, Seward Mer.; 60°32'42" N, 148°26'50" W. BGN 8002.

CRANBERRY LAKE	lake, 0.8 km. (0.5 mi.) long, 2.4 km. (1.5 mi.) S of Big Lake; sec. 11, T 16 N, R 4 W, Seward Mer.; 61°29'40" N, 149°56'15" W. BGN 7304.
CRAVENS PEAK	peak, elevation 1,884 m. (6,180 ft.), in the Brooks Range 43 km. (27 mi.) W of Survey Pass; named for Larry Frank Cravens (1941-1972), guide and sportsman and smoke jumper for the Bureau of Land Management; 67°48'47" N, 155°09'33" W. BGN 7401.
CRESCENT ISLAND	island, 1.6 km. (1 mi.) long in the Plover Islands between Deadmans and Doctor Islands 7 km. (4.4 mi.) SE of Point Barrow; 71°21'35" N, 156°18'00" W. Variants: Deadmans Island, Doctor Island. BGN 7504.
Crescent Island	island, see Doctor Island.
Crested Point	point of land, see Tsimpshian Point.
Cribbee Creek	stream, see Cribby Creek.
CRIBBY CREEK	stream, 5.5 mi. long, heads at 61°50'45" N, 157°20'20" W, flows SE to the Kuskokwim River 1.3 mi. N of Red Devil; 61°46'53" N, 157°18'30" W. Not: Cribbee Creek (former decision). BGN 1943. BGN 1967.
CROOKED LAKE	lake, 2.2 km. (1.4 mi.) long, 37 km. (23 mi.) NW of Anchorage; Matanuska-Susitna Borough; secs. 31 and 32, T 17 N, R 4 W, Seward Mer.; 61°31'15" N, 150°02'40" W; 1978 decision revised. Not: Finger Lake (BGN 1978). BGN 7904.
Crow Island	island, see Gull Island.
CROWN PEAK	peak, elevation over 5,900 ft., on the crown of the glaciers on Kenai Peninsula 27 mi. NE of Seward; 60°19'10" N, 148°46'08" W. BGN 1929. BGN 1968.

CROWN REEFER POINT	point of land, 0.3 mi. wide in the Aleutian Islands, on the N coast of Amchitka Island 5.7 mi. NW of Kirilof Point; named for the salvage ship *Crown Reefer* wrecked here shortly after World War II; 51°28'07" N, 179°11'30" E. BGN 1969.
CRYSTALLINE HILLS	hills, 16 mi. long, highest elevation 6,510 ft., between the Gilahina River, on the N, and Lakina and Chitina Rivers, on the S, 12 mi. W of McCarthy; 61°25'45" N, 143°41'20" W (W end), 61°26'45" N, 143°15'00" W (E end). BGN 1969.
CUL-DE-SAC GLACIER	glacier, 7 mi. long, heads on the Cathedral Spires at 62°25'00" N, 152°44'20" W, trends NNW, between Tatina and Shelf Glaciers, to a point 1 mi. S of Shellabarger Pass; 62°30'48" N,, 152°47'00" W. Not: Cool Sac Glacier. BGN 1969.
Culkana River	stream, see Gulkana River.
Culkena River	stream, see Gulkana River.
CURVE CREEK	stream, 22.5 km. (14 mi.) long, heads at 69°16'50" N, 145°33'35" W, flows NW to Eagle Creek 14.5 km. (9 mi.) SE of Mount Copleston; stream has several arcuate bends; 69°24'10" N, 145°53'00" W. BGN 7601.
CYGNET LAKE	lake, 1.1 km. (0.7 mi.) long, 3.2 km. (2 mi.) W of the Chulitna River and 19.3 km. (12 mi.) NNW of Talkeetna; secs. 35 and 36, T 28 N, R 6 W, Seward Mer.; 62°28'15" N, 150°19'00" W. BGN 8001.
CYRIL COVE	cove, 0.3 mi. across, on the N coast of Amchitka Island 4 mi. NW of Kirilof Point; 51°26'35" N, 179°12'35" E. Not: Kirilof Cove. 1944. BGN 1973.
Cyril Cove	cove, see Square Bay.

Daiye	locality, see Dyea.
Dall Mountain	mountain, see Langille Mountain.
DAVIDSON BAY	bay, 2.1 km. (1.3 mi.) across, on E side of Keku Strait 1.6 km. (1 mi.) SE of Dakaneek Bay and 16 km. (10 mi.) SE of Kake; named for the National Oceanic and Atmospheric Administration ship <u>Davidson</u> which anchored in the bay for three summers while working in the Keku Strait area; T 58 S, Rgs. 73 and 74 E, Copper River Mer.; 56°50'28" N, 133°51'00" W. BGN 7704.
DAVIS LAKE	lake, 2.4 km. (1.5 mi.) long, drains NW to Port Wells, 2.4 km. (1.5 mi.) W of Cap Glacier and 45 km. (28 mi.) NE of Whittier; secs. 11, 13, and 14, T 10 N, R 8 E, Seward Mer.; 60°57'30" N, 147°57'30" W. BGN 8003.
DAWN LAKE	lake, 0.4 km. (0.25 mi.) long, 7.2 km. (4.5 mi.) E of Big Lake and 14.5 km. (9 mi.) W of Wasilla; sec. 19, T 17 N, R 2 W, Seward Mer.; 61°32'42" N, 149°42'00" W. BGN 8001.
Dayay	locality, see Dyea.
DAYVILLE	locality, on S shore of Swanport on S side of Port Valdez 6 km. (3.7 mi.) SW of Valdez; 61°05'10" N, 146°24'00" W. Variant: Swanport. BGN 7504.
De Long Lake	lake, see Longmere Lake.
Deadman Island	island, see Doctor Island.
DEADMANS ISLAND	island, 0.5 km. (0.3 mi.) long, in the Plover Islands between Elson Lagoon and the Beaufort Sea 8.4 km. (5.2 mi.) SE of Point Barrow; 71°21'15" N, 156°16'30" W. Variant: Doctor Island. BGN 7504.
Deadmans Island	island, see Crescent Island.
Deadmans Island	island, see Tapkaluk Islands.

DECEPTION CREEK	stream, 3 mi. long, on Montague Island, heads at 59°50'15" N, 147°43'15" W, flows SW to the Gulf of Alaska 2.7 mi. W of Neck Point: 59°48'12" N, 147°45'20" W. BGN 1967.
Deep Bay	bay, see Sea Otter Bay.
DEER CREEK	stream, 0.5 mi. long, on Baranof Island, heads at E end of Deer Lake, flows E to Mist Cove 20 mi. N of Port Alexander; 56°31'10" N, 134°40'10" W. Not: Deer Lake Outlet. BGN 1968.
Deer Lake Outlet	stream, see Deer Creek.
Dejah	locality, see Dyea.
DELIVERANCE, MOUNT	mountain, elevation 2,411 m. (7,910 ft.) in the Romanzof Mountains 7 km. (4.4 mi.) NE of Mount Hubley and 20.9 km. (13 mi.) ENE of Mount Michelson; sec. 20, T 1 S, R 35 E, Umiat Mer.; 69°20'05" N, 143°44'10". Not: Mount Waw. BGN 7902.
Delyndia Lake	lake, see Butterfly Lake.
Delyndia Lake	lake, see East Butterfly Lake.
DENALI, LAKE	lake, 1.9 km. (1.2 mi.) long, 21 km. (13 mi.) NNW of Talkeetna; secs. 23 and 26, T 28 N, R 6 W, Seward Mer.; 62°29'20" N, 150°19'45" W. BGN 7403.
DERBY COVE	cove, 0.16 km. (0.1 mi.) across, on the W shore of Resurrection Bay on the Kenai Peninsula, 8 km. (5 mi.) S of Seward; Kenai Peninsula Borough; sec. 3, T 2 S, R 1 W, Seward Mer.; 60°01'52" N, 149°26'23" W. BGN 8003.
DEVILS PASS	pass, at W end of Gilpatrick Mountain, 5.5 mi. NE of Juneau Lake and 36 mi. NNW of Seward; 60°36'30" N, 149°43'00" W. 1966. BGN 1967.
DEVILS PASS LAKE	lake, 0.4 mi. long, 4 mi. E of Swan Lake and 36 mi. NNW of Seward; 60°36'50" N, 149°43'30" W. 1966. BGN 1967.
Devils Rock	rock, see Hub Rock.

DEVILS THUMB	peak, elevation 1,600 m. (5,250 ft.), between Trims Creek and Castner Glacier 12.9 km. (8 mi.) SE of Black Rapids; sec. 20, T 17 S, R 11 E, Fairbanks Mer.; 63°25'40" N, 145°41'25" W. Variant: Devils Thumbs. BGN 7702.
Devils Thumbs	peak, see Devils Thumb.
DICKINSON GLACIER	glacier, 2 mi. long, heads on the N side of Takhinsha Mountains, trends N to its terminus 1.4 mi. S of the Takhin River and 17.5 mi. W of Haines; local name given for the wife of George Dickinson, agent for the Northwest Trading Company at Haines in 1878; 59°13' N, 135°56' W. BGN 1967.
Diomede	locality, see Inalik.
DOCTOR ISLAND	island, 0.3 km. (0.2 mi.) long, at the NW end of the Plover Islands between Elson Lagoon and the Beaufort Sea 6 km. (3.8 mi.) SE of Point Barrow; 71°21'40" N, 156°20'25" W; 1916 description revised. Variants: Crescent Island, Deadman Island, Deadmans Island, Doctors Island, Il-luit-kuk, Martin Island. BGN 7504.
Doctor Island	island, see Crescent Island.
Doctors Island	island, see Doctor Island.
Dog Bay	bay, see Saint Herman Bay.
Dog Salmon Bay	bay, see Koyuktolik Bay.
Dogfish Bay	bay, see Koyuktolik Bay.
DOGGIE ISLAND	island, 3.5 km. (2.2 mi.) long, in Yakutat Bay 5.4 km. (3.4 mi.) NE of Yakutat; this name, probably derived from the Russian word "dolgoi" meaning "long", is the result of folk etymology; 59°36'15" N, 139°41'00" W. Variant: Dolgoi Island. BGN 7702.
DOGSLED PASS	pass, elevation over 4,200 ft., in the Talkeetna Mountains, between the headwaters of Craigie and Purches Creeks 16 mi. NNW of Palmer; 61°48'50" N, 149°18'15" W. BGN 1969.

Dolgoi Island | island, see Doggie Island.

DOLOMITE CREEK | stream, 11.3 km. (7 mi.) long, heads 11.3 km. (7 mi.) SW of Stone Mountain at 63°39'30" N, 154°01'50" W, flows NNW to Browns Fork 15.3 km. (9.5 mi.) E of Lone Indian Mountain and 75 km. (47 mi.) NNE of Medfra; named for mountains composed of dolomite in the headwaters; sec. 25, T 20 S, R 24 E, Keteel River Mer.; 63°43'57" N, 154°06'12" W. BGN 8402.

DON SHELDON AMPHITHEATER | basin, 11.3 km. (7 mi.) long, 16 km. (10 mi.) SE of the summit of Mount McKinley at the head of Ruth Glacier N of the Great Gorge; named for Donald E. Sheldon (1921-1975), bush pilot who flew over 27 years in support of mapping, patrol, mountaineering, search and rescue, and wildlife air census operations on and in the area of Mount McKinley; T 22 S, Rgs. 16 and 17 W, Fairbanks Mer.; 63°00'00" N, 150°42'00" W. Variants: Ruth Amphitheater, Ruth Amphitheatre. BGN 7501.

Douglas Island | island, see Douglass Island.

DOUGLASS ISLAND | island, 0.64 km. (0.4) mi. long, in Cordova Bay 4.8 km. (3 mi.) NW of Point Marsh; named for Chief Douglass of the Hyda Indians who lived on the island; 54°45'30" N, 132°20'40" W. Variant: Douglas Island. BGN 7504.

DOWNDRAFT LAKE | lake, 0.6 mi. long on Gravina Island 12 mi. SW of Ketchikan; this name is derived from the turbulent down drafts created by the steep mountains around the lake; 55°12'15" N, 131°47'15" W. BGN 1972.

DRAIN CREEK | stream, 30 km. (19 mi.) long, heads at 69°05'25" N, 142°38'35" W, flows E to Kongakut River 24 km. (15 mi.) SW of Mount Greenough; 69°01'45" N, 142°06'20" W. BGN 7501.

Dry Creek | village, see Healy.

DUBIN BAY	bight, 29 km. (18 mi.) across, extends NE from Cape Sarichef to Cave Point on the W coast of Unimak Island in the Aleutian Islands; 54°42'00" N, 164°45'00" W. BGN 7603.
DUCK COVE	cove, 0.64 km. (0.4 mi.) across, on the S coast of Amchitka Island 3.2 km. (2 mi.) NW of Makarius Bay; 51°24'50" N, 179°09'30" E. BGN 7504.
DUNCAN SLOUGH	cove, 0.48 km. (0.3 mi.) long, on the S shore of Port Graham, 0.97 km. (0.6 mi.) SSE of the village of Port Graham and 12.3 km. (7.6 mi.) SW of Seldovia; Kenai Peninsula Borough; NW 1/4, sec. 4, T 10 S, R 15 W, Seward Mer.; 59°20'37" N, 151°49'20" W. BGN 8203.
Dununak	village, see Tununak.
Dununuk	village, see Tununak.
DYEA	locality, in Klondike Gold Rush National Historic Park, site of former Chilkat Tlingit Indian village, on W bank of the Taiya River 5.6 km. (3.5 mi.) NNW of Skagway; sec. 27, T 27 S, R 59 E, Copper River Mer.; 59°30'17" N, 135°21'30" W; 1898 description revised. Not: Daiye, Dayay, Dejah, Taiya, Tyya. BGN 8404.

EAGLE LAKE	lake, 4 mi. long, at the head of the Eagle River, 43 mi. SE of Wrangell; 56°02'45" N, 131°27'30" W. 1955. BGN 1966.
EAST ALAPAH GLACIER	glacier, 1.8 mi. long, heads on Alapah Mountain at 68°07'50" N, 150°50'00" W, trends NNE to the head of an unnamed tributary of the Nanushuk River 3 mi. W of Cockedhat Mountain; 68°08'55" N, 150°48'15" W. BGN 1969.
East Arm Nuka Bay	fiord, see McCarty Fiord.
EAST BUTTERFLY LAKE	lake, 2.4 km. (1.5 mi.) long, 43 km. (27 mi.) NW of Anchorage; Matanuska-Susitna Borough; Tps. 17 and 18 N, Rgs. 4 and 5 W, Seward Mer.; 61°36'00" N, 150°05'00" W; 1968 decision revised. Not: Butterfly Lake, Delyndia Lake (BGN 1968). BGN 7902.
East Butterfly Lake	lake, see Butterfly Lake.
EAST CRATER	crater, 0.64 km. (0.4 mi.) across, on Mount Wrangell 1.3 km. (0.8 mi.) E of its summit and 4 km. (2.5 mi.) ENE of Wrangell Crater; secs. 29 and 32, T 3 N, R 8 E, Copper River Mer.; 62°00'12" N, 143°59'35" W. BGN 8002.
EAST FINGER INLET	inlet, 3.2 km. (2 mi.) long, on Kenai Peninsula, opens to Port Nellie Juan 4 km. (2.5 mi.) E of Coxcomb Point; secs. 2, 3, and 10, T 5 N, and sec. 35, T 6 N, R 6 E, Seward Mer.; 60°32'30" N, 148°22'20" W. BGN 8002.
East Fork Chena River	stream, see Middle Fork.
EAST FORK SAWMILL CREEK	stream, 1.1 km. (0.7 mi.) long, heads at 61°44'45" N, 149°31'00" W, flows N to join the West Fork to form Sawmill Creek 20.1 km. (12.5 mi.) NNW of Wasilla; Matanuska-Susitna Borough; sec. 6, T 19 N, R 1 W, Seward Mer.; 61°45'40" N, 149°31'30" W. Not: Sawmill Creek. BGN 7902.

EAST NULARVIK CREEK	stream, 3.2 km. (2 mi.) long, heads at 69°38'05" N, 144°58'35" W, flows W to Nularvik River 6.4 km. (4 mi.) W of Mount Weller; sec. 5, T 3 N, R 29 E, Umiat Mer.; 69°38'25" N, 145°03'25" W. BGN 7501.
EAST REDCLIFF ISLAND	island, 0.97 km. (0.6 mi.) long, one of the Redcliff Islands, in Freshwater Bay, 14.5 km. (9 mi.) NE of the village of Tenakee Springs; 57°53'38" N, 135°05'40" W. BGN 8103.
Eastern Shoal	shoal, see Tzuse Shoal.
EDES LAKE	lake, 1.3 mi. long, in Broad Pass .5 mi. NE of Summit Lake and 6 mi. SW of Cantwell; named for William C. Edes (1856-1922), chief engineer and chairman, Alaskan Engineering Commission (1914-1920); 63°19'45" N, 149°05'30" W; 1927 description revised. Variant: Lake Edes. BGN 7303.
Egg Island	island, see Gull Island.
Eichholz Pass	pass, see Guilbeau Pass.
Eleanor Island	island, see Tla-xagh Island.
ELLISON, MOUNT	mountain, elevation 697 m. (2,288 ft.), on Kodiak Island 4.2 km. (2.6 mi.) N of Port Lions; named for Carl Oscar Ellison, Jr. (1920-1972), under whose leadership as president of the Village Council of Afognak, the population moved to Port Lions after the 1964 earthquake and tidal wave; sec. 20, T 26 S, R 22 W, Seward Mer.; 57°54'20" N, 152°52'10" W. BGN 7403.
Elovoi	point of land, see Ouzinkie Point.
Emanguk	village, see Emmonak.
EMERALD LAKE	lake, 0.25 mi. long, in the Aleutian Islands, on Amchitka Island 2 mi. S of Sea Otter Point; named for the abnormal green color of the water; 51°29'42" N, 179°03'40" E. BGN 1969.

EMERY TOBIN, LAKE	lake, 0.32 km. (0.2 mi.) long, at the head of Lunch Creek 16.1 km. (10 mi.) N of Ketchikan; named for Emery F. Tobin (?-1977), publisher and editor of the *Alaska Sportsman* magazine; Ketchikan Gateway Borough, sec. 36, T 73 S, R 90 E, Copper River Mer.; 55°29'32" N, 131°39'25" W. BGN 7901.
EMIL LAKE	lake, 0.3 mi. long, 16 mi. SSE of Talkeetna; named for Emil Rokita, who owned property on the shore of the lake; 62°06'10" N, 149°59'00" W. BGN 1969.
EMMONAK	village, on the N bank of Kwiguk Pass 7 mi. NE of Alakanuk; 62°46'35" N, 164°31'40" W. Variants: Emanguk, Emonguk. BGN 7303.
Emonguk	village, see Emmonak.
Entrance Island	island, see Entrance Islet.
ENTRANCE ISLET	island, 0.16 km. (0.1 mi.) across, in the Necker Islands, at W point of entrance to Symonds Bay off N coast of Biorka Island 24 km. (15 mi.) SW of Sitka; 56°51'55" N, 135°31'20" W. Not: Entrance Island. BGN 7801.
ERNEST GRUENING, MOUNT	peak, elevation 1,833 m. (6,015 ft.), in the Coast Mountains 32 km. (20 mi.) NW of Juneau; named for Ernest Gruening (died 1974), former Alaska Governor and U.S. Senator; sec. 22, T 38 S, R 65 E, Copper River Mer.; 58°34'10" N, 134°39'10" W; 1968 decision revised. Variants: Goat Mountain, Mount Adolph Knopf (former decision). BGN 7602.
ESKA CREEK	stream, 12.9 km. (8 mi.) long, heads at 61°47'30" N, 148°56'30" W, on Eska Mountain, flows S to the Matanuska River 4 km. (2.5 mi.) SSW of Eska; sec. 28, T 19 N, R 3 E, Seward Mer.; 61°42'15" N, 148°55'01" W. Not: Knob Creek. BGN 7801.
Esker Island	island, see Gull Island.

ESKILIDA CREEK — stream, 3.7 km. (2.3 mi.) long, heads at 61°27'22" N, 144°31'23" W, flows E to the Copper River 6.4 km. (4 mi.) S of Chitina; named for the Eskilida family which formerly had a settlement at the mouth of the stream: 61°27'18" N, 144°27'18" W. BGN 7401.

EULACHON RIVER — stream, 7 mi. long, heads at 56°10'40" N, 131°08'10" W, flows SSE to the Unuk River at Burroughs Bay; 56°05'17" N, 131°05'33" W. Not: Huiakan River, Hulakan River, Hulakin River, Hulakon River (former decision). BGN 1923. BGN 1969.

EWE GLACIER — glacier, 4.5 mi. long, heads at 61°03'45" N, 141°15'25" W, trends S for 2 mi., then NW, to a point 0.2 mi. E of Ram Glacier and 5 mi. SW of Mount Tittmann; 61°03'40" N, 141°21'20" W. BGN 1967.

EXIT GLACIER — glacier, 6.4 km. (4 mi.) long, in Kenai Fjords National Park, heads in the Harding Ice Field and trends ENE to an unnamed tributary of the Resurrection River 14.5 km. (9 mi.) NW of Seward; so named because it is the location of the "exit" of the first recorded party to cross the Harding Ice Field in 1968; Kenai Peninsula Borough; 60°11'00" N, 149°37'32" W. BGN 8203.

FACE MOUNTAIN	mountain, elevation 1,707 m. (5,600 ft.), near head of Taiya Inlet 6.7 km. (4.2 mi.) WNW of Skagway; sec. 6, T 28 S, R 59 E, Copper River Mer.; 59°28'40" N, 135°25'45" W. Not: Gnome Mountain, Parsons Peak, The Sphinx. BGN 8504.
Faith Lake	lake, see Liten Lake.
FALLING WATER CREEK	stream, 5.6 km. (3.5 mi.) long, heads at an unnamed glacier 2.4 km. (1.5 mi.) W of Peekaboo Peak at 61°16'34" N, 149°14'20" W, flows SW to a branch of Eagle River 32 km. (20 mi.) E of Anchorage; descriptive name; Municipality of Anchorage; sec. 4, T 13 N, R 1 E, Seward Mer.; 61°14'42" N, 149°17'45" W. BGN 8203.
FALLS CREEK	stream, 1.8 mi. long, in the Aleutian Islands, heads at 51°30'52" N, 179°01'56" E, flows SW to the Pacific Ocean on the S coast of Amchitka Island; named for the waterfall near its mouth; 51°30'02" N, 179°00'54" E. BGN 1969.
Fankuda Island	island, see Fankuda Islet.
FANKUDA ISLET	island, 0.32 km. (0.2 mi.) across, in Redoubt Bay off W coast of Baranof Island 8.4 km. (5.2 mi.) N of Goddard; named "Ostsrov Fankuda" (meaning Fankuda Island or Islet) in 1809 by the Russian navigator, Ivan Vasiliev, the first, and published in 1826 by Lt. G. A. Sarichev, of the Imperial Russian Navy; 56°54'35" N, 135°21'35" W. Not: Fankuda Island, Ostrov Fankuda. BGN 7801.
FAULT COVE	cove, 0.7 mi. long, on W coast of Montague Island 2 mi. NE of Point Woodcock; formed by fault movement during the 1964 earthquake; 59°55'38" N, 147°46'15" W. BGN 1967.

FERRIC CREEK	stream, 3.5 mi. long, heads at 68°07'00" N, 163°12'55" W, flows S to the Sulik River 2 mi. S of Punupkahkroak Mountain; feature cuts a sulfide-bearing rock formation which supplies iron to coat the stream bed; sec. 22, T 31 N, R 20 W, Kateel River Mer.; 68°04'23" N, 163°11'55" W. BGN 1972.

FIN COVE	bay, 2.6 km. (1.6 mi.) across, on Chichagof Island, along the S shore of Tenakee Inlet between Trap and Corner Bays, 7.4 km. (4.6 mi.) SE of Tenakee Springs; City and Borough of Sitka; 57°45'20" N, 135°05'00" W. BGN 8203.

Finger Islands	shoal, see Finger Shoal.

Finger Islets	shoal, see Finger Shoal.

Finger Lake	lake, see Crooked Lake.

FINGER SHOAL	shoal, 0.64 km. (0.4 mi.) long, in Sumner Strait, off W coast of Kosciusko Island at S entrance to Shipley Bay 0.97 km. (0.6 mi.) N of Ruins Point and 32 km. (20 mi.) S of Point Baker; T 67 S, R 76 E, Copper River Mer.; 56°04'30" W, 133°42'07" W; 1978 decision revised. Not: Finger Islands (BGN 1978); Finger Islets. BGN 8104.

FINNBEAR LAKE	lake, 1.6 km. (1 mi.) long, in Happy River Valley 4.3 km. (2.7 mi.) S of Columbia Peak and 129 km. (80 mi.) WSW of Talkeetna; named for nearby mining claims on the N shore of the lake that have been in opertaion since the mid-1960's; secs. 7 8, and 17, T 22 N, R 17 W, Seward Mer.; 62°00'30" N, 152°26'30" W. BGN 7901.

FIRE ISLAND SHOAL	shoal, 10.7 km. (6.6 mi.) long, in Cook Inlet, 8 km. (5 mi.) W of Fire Island and 40 km. (25 mi.) ENE of Tyonek; 61°09'46" N, 150°18'46" W (NE end), 61°08'14" N, 150°25'22" W (SW end). BGN 8103.

FIRESTONE CREEK	stream, 4 mi. long, heads at 68°17'00" N, 151°48'05" W, flows NW to Tiglukpuk Creek 9 mi. N of Soakpak Mountain; firestone is the local term used for rocks found in the stream; 68°19'15" N, 151°52'15" W. BGN 1972.
FISH CREEK	stream, 15 mi. long, heads in Fish Lake at 65°02'47" N, 151°21'10" W, flows NW to the Tanana River 15 mi. SE of Tanana; 65°04'45" N, 151°37'45" W. Not: Boulder Creek (former decision, in part), Guthna Creek. 1908. BGN 1968.
FISH ISLAND	island, 0.48 km. (0.3 mi.) long, in the Gulf of Alaska, at E end of Wooded Islands off SE coast of Montague Island 9.1 km. (5.6 mi.) S of Box Point; sec. 26, T 3 S, R 12 E, Seward Mer.; 59°52'55" N, 147°20'30" W. BGN 7803.
Fishook Lake	lake, see Anderson Lake.
Fishook Lake	lake, see Kings Lake.
Flattop Mountain	mountain see Three Step Mountain.
FLINTS POINT	point of land, on the E coast of Chichagof Island 35 mi. SW of Juneau; named for George M. Flint, Jr. (1918-1965), geologist and coordination and liaison officer with the Alaska Branch of the U.S. Geological Survey for 23 years, who did geological field work in this area; 57°54'25" N, 134°57'53" W. BGN 1968.
FLUTE GLACIER	glacier, 2.1 mi. long, heads at 61°07'48" N, 149°17'15" W, trends N to the head of the South Fork Eagle River 20 mi. ESE of Anchorage; 61°09'39" N, 149°17'22" W. BGN 1969.
FOLDED TOWERS	peaks, two on a serrated ridge 0.8 mi. apart, higher elevation over 6,700 ft., 1.2 mi. SW of The Snow Towers and 22.5 mi. NNW of Juneau; the name is descriptive; sec. 32, T 37 S, R 66 E, Copper River Mer.; 58°37'12" N, 134°32'30" W (at higher point). BGN 1971.

FOREMOST ROCK   rock, in Sumner Strait, S of Woewodski Island and 3.5 km. (2.2 mi.) WSW of Point Alexander; T 62 S, R 79 E, Copper River Mer.; 56°30'08" N, 133°00'13" W. BGN 8203.

FORESTA, MOUNT   peak, approximate elevation 3,444 m. (11,300 ft.) in the Saint Elias Mountains, 18.5 km. (11.5 mi.) NW of Mount Seattle and 74 km. (46 mi.) N of Yakutat; named for Foresta H. Wood (1904-1951) who was responsible for the logistic planning of Project Snow Cornice of the Arctic Institute of North America and who, with her daughter, was killed in an airplane crash in the area of this mountain; T 21 S, R 35 E, Copper River Mer.; 60°11'30" N, 139°26'00" W; 1960 description revised. BGN 8001.

Fort Island   island, see Gull Island.

FOSSIL CREEK   stream, 4.8 km. (3 mi.) long, heads at 69°35'02" N, 145°06'55" W, flows S to Fire Creek 16.1 km. (10 mi.) SW of Mount Weller; stream cuts through fossiliferous rocks; sec. 7, T 2 N, R 29 E, Umiat Mer.; 69°32'34" N, 145°05'55" W. BGN 7501.

FOSTER, MOUNT   hill, elevation 405 m. (1,329 ft.), on the Seward Peninsula, E of Hannum Creek, 34 km. (21 mi.) SW of Deering; named for Neal Winston Foster (?-1979), the State's first Director of Air Commerce, a member of the Territorial and State Legislatures, and who developed mining claims on nearby Hannum Creek; secs. 20, 21, 28 and 29, T 6 N, R 22 W, Kateel River Mer.; 65°53'25" N, 163°20'33" W. BGN 8301.

FOUR FALLS LAKE   lake, 1.5 mi. long, on Baranof Island 22 mi. ESE of Sitka; 57°00'00" N, 134°46'30" W. BGN 1969.

FOURTH OF JULY CREEK   stream, 8 km. (5 mi.) long, heads at an unnamed glacier at 60°05'15" N, 149°14'20" W, flows W to Resurrection Bay 4.8 km. (3 mi.) SE of Seward; sec. 18, T 1 S, R 1 E, Seward Mer.; 60°05'22" N, 149°21'15" W. BGN 8401.

FOX ISLAND   island, 5.6 km. (3.5 mi.) long, W of Resurrection Peninsula between Eldorado Narrows and Resurrection Bay, 4 km. (2.5 mi.) NNW of Cape Resurrection; Kenai Peninsula Borough; T 3 S, R 1 E and R 1 W, Seward Mer.; 59°55'10" N, 149°20'00" W; 1906 decision revised. Not: Lowell Island, Renard Island (BGN 1906). BGN 8003.

FRANKLIN CREEK   stream, 30 km. (19 mi.) long, heads at 69°07'00" N, 145°06'25" W, flows W to the Canning River 19.3 km. (12 mi.) E of Mount Salisbury; 69°09'30" N, 145°46'20" W. BGN 7501.

FRENCH JOE MOUNTAIN   hill, elevation 555 m. (1,822 ft.), in the Kuskokwim Mountains, 15.3 km. (9.5 mi.) NNW of Mount Joaquin and 14.5 km. (9 mi.) W of Takotna, named for Louis Blackburn (French Joe), gold prospector in the Innoko mining area; sec. 32, T 34 N, R 37 W, Seward Mer.; 62°59'33" N, 156°20'55" W. BGN 8402.

FRITTS MOUNTAIN   mountain, elevation, 1,453 m. (4,765 ft.), at the W end of the Angayucham Mountains 83 km. (52 mi.) NNE of Hogatza; named for Dr. Crawford E. Fritts (deceased 1972), who spent four seasons mapping the geology of the southern Brooks Range, including two seasons in the Angayucham Mountains; 66°55'30" N, 155°30'00" W. BGN 7403.

FRYING PAN LAKE   lake, 0.81 km. (0.5 mi.) across, 0.97 km. (0.6 mi.) NE of Nancy; secs. 26, 27, 34, and 35, T 19 N, R 4 W, Seward Mer; 61°42'00" N, 149°57'33" W. BGN 7702.

FUMAROLE COVE   cove, 0.35 mi. across, in the Aleutian Islands, along the S coast of Amchitka Island 0.6 mi. SE of White House Cove; named for Fumarole Valley which ends at this cove; 51°33'30" N, 178°53'45" E. BGN 1969.

FUMAROLE VALLEY valley, 2.5 mi. long, in the Aleutian islands, crosses Amchitka Island from Chitka Cove, on the NE, to Fumarole Cove, on the SW; named for the many bleached areas of rock, thought to be extinct fumaroles; 51°35'10" N, 178°55'50" E (NE end), 51°33'50" N, 178°53'50" E (SW end). BGN 1969.

GAILEY CREEK	stream, 13.7 km. (8.5 mi.) long, heads at 66°51'58" N, 144°14'26" W, flows SW through Gailey Lake to Sheenjek River 46 km. (28 mi.) NE of Fort Yukon; sec. 23, T 23 N, R 15 E, Fairbanks Mer.; 66°48'00" N, 144°25'22" W. BGN 8301.
Gar Lake	lake, see Maksoutof Lake.
GIANTS HEAD	promontory, 1.1 km. (0.7 mi.) across, extends N into Skowl Arm on E coast of Prince of Wales Island 43 km. (27 mi.) WNW of Ketchikan; shape of the feature resembles a head; secs. 34 and 35, T 74 S, R 86 E, Copper River Mer.; 55°24'40" N, 132°18'30" W. Not: Giants Head Point. BGN 9702.
Giants Head Point	promontory, see Giants Head.
GIL HARBOR	bay, 1.6 km. (1 mi.) across, on W side of Keku Strait 16 km. (10 mi.) SSW of Kake; T 58 S and Rgs. 72 and 73 E, Copper River Mer.; 56°50'10" N, 133°59'20" W. BGN 7702.
Gilbert Island	peninsula, see Gilbert Peninsula.
Gilbert Lake	lake, see Lower Sweetheart Lake.
GILBERT PENINSULA	peninsula, 6.5 mi. long, in Glacier Bay 3.5 mi. S of Composite Island; 58°48'30" N, 136°34'00" W, 1937 decision revised. Not: Gilbert Island (former decision). BGN 1972.
GISEL PEAK	peak, elevation 7,532 ft., on Alaska-Canada boundary 35 mi. NE of Juneau; named for Charles Alonzo Gisel (1926-1967), helicopter pilot who supported many scientific parties in the Juneau Icefield region; 58°46'03" N, 133°58'15" W. Not: Boundary Peak 94. BGN 1968.
GLACIER CREEK	stream, 1.9 km. (1.2 mi.) long, heads at 63°42'03" N, 160°49'00" W, flows NW to Norton Sound between Cascade and Coal Mine Creeks 19.3 km. (12 mi.) S of Unalakleet; sec. 33, T 20 S, R 11 W, Kateel River Mer.; 63°42'28" N, 160°50'30" W. BGN 8103.

Glacier Creek	stream, see Coal Mine Creek.
Glacier Creek	stream, see Jesse Creek.
GNARLED MOUNTAIN	mountain, 3 mi. long, highest elevation 1,975 ft., 18 mi. W of Dillingham; T 13 S, R 58 W, Seward Mer.; 59°01'40" N, 158°58'05" W. BGN 1972.
Gnome Mountain	mountain, see Face Mountain.
Goat Mountain	peak, see Ernest Gruening, Mount.
Goat Mountain	mountain, see Langille Mountain.
GOLGOTHA	mountain, elevation 8,940 ft., in Revelation Mountains 11 mi. WNW of Mount Mausolus; 61°39'35" N, 154°10'10" W. BGN 1968.
GOLUB, MOUNT	mountain, elevation 4,194 ft., 4 mi. SE of Nun Mountain and 14 mi. W of Dotsons Landing; named for Harvey Golub (1930-1971), member of the party which made the first recorded climb of this mountain in 1968; sec. 28, T 39 S, R 62 E, Copper River Mer.; 58°27'50" N, 135°10'15" W. BGN 1972.
Good News Bay	populated place, see Goodnews Bay.
GOODNEWS BAY	populated place (incorporated city), on the N shore of Goodnews Bay at the mouth of the Goodnews River 69 km. (43 mi.) WNW of Togiak; incorporated as Goodnews Bay July 9, 1970; sec. 21, T 12 S, R 73 W, Seward Mer.; 59°07'08" N, 161°35'15" W; 1939 decision revised. Not: Goodnews (former decision), Good News Bay, Mumtrahamut, Mumtrahamute, Mumtrak, Mumtrakmut. BGN 7802.
GOSSAN RIDGE	ridge, 1 mi. long, highest elevation 975 ft., 38 mi. SE of Candle; name derived from the gossans that are found on the ridge; 65°25'00" N, 161°21'15" W (S end). BGN 1969.
GRAMPUS POINT	point of land, in the Aleutian Islands, southernmost point on Amchitka Island 1.5 mi. SE of Saint Makarius Point; 51°21'00" N, 179°14'18" E. Not: Saint Makarius Point. BGN 1969.

GRAND PARAPET, THE	ridge, 2 mi. long, at the head of Chitistone Glacier in the University Range, 10 mi. NW of University Peak and 28 mi. E. of McCarthy; 61°24'40" N, 142°01'30" W (E end), 61°24'35" N, 142°04'30" W (W end). BGN 1967.
GRAPTOLITE CANYON	canyon, 4.8 km. (3 mi.) long, in the Terra Cotta Mountains, heads at 62°12'35" N, 153°33'25" W, trends SE to a tributary valley of the South Fork Kuskokwim River 3.2 km. (2 mi.) NE of Post Lake; named for the abundance of graptolite fossils found at the head of the canyon; sec. 10, T 24 N, R 23 W, Seward Mer.; 62°10'40" N, 153°28'40" W. BGN 8202.
GRASSY LAKE	lake, 0.48 km. (0.3 mi.) across, 1.6 km. (1 mi.) S of Ryan Lake and 5.1 km. (3.2 mi.) SE of Unalakleet; secs. 13 and 24, T 19 S, R 11 W, Kateel River Mer.; 63°50'10" N, 160°43'45" W. Not: Ryan Lake. BGN 8103.
Grayline Lake	lake, see Grayling Lake.
GRAYLING LAKE	lake, 0.4 mi. long, 1.5 mi. E of Lost Lake and 10 mi. NNE of Seward; 60°16'20" N, 149°22'20" W. 1964. BGN 1968.
GRAYLING LAKE	lake,, 1.1 km. (0.7 mi.) long, in the Brooks Range 2.9 km. (1.8 mi.) NW of Arctic Village; named for the fish that are found in the lake; secs. 11 and 12, T 15 S, R 28 E, Umiat Mer.; 68°09'20" N. 145°34'20" W. Variant: Grayline Lake. BGN 7603.
GREEN HILL	hill, elevation 461 m. (1,312 ft.), N of Kushtaka Lake; secs. 1, 12, and 13, T 17 S, R 7 E, and secs. 6, 7, and 18, T 17 S, R 8 E, Copper River Mer.; 60°24'55" N, 144°04'20" W. BGN 7504.
GREYSTONE BAY	bay, 1.6 km. (1 mi.) across, on Kenai Peninsula on S shore of Port Nellie Juan 2.4 km. (1.5 mi.) SE of Coxcomb Point; secs. 16 and 17, T 5 N, R 6 E, Seward Mer.; 60°31'30" N, 148°25'30" W. BGN 8002.

GUILBEAU PASS   pass, in the Brooks Range 104 km. (65 mi.) NNE of Arctic Village; named for Samuel Guilbeau (1945-1972), who died in the vicinity of the pass during a one-man geological reconnaissance; 68°57'20" N, 144°26'45" W. Variant: Eichholz Pass. BGN 7504.

Gulkana Creek   stream, see Gulkana River.

Gulkana Creek   stream, see Phelan Creek.

GULKANA RIVER   stream, 50 mi. long, heads at the SE end of Summit Lake at 63°06'25" N, 145°29'45" W, flows S to the Copper River 9 mi. NE of Glennallen; 63°13'15" N, 145°23'10" W. Not: Culkana River, Culkena River, Gulkana Creek, Gulkena River, Kulkana River, Tonkina River. 1899. BGN 1969.

Gulkana River   stream, see Phelan Creek.

Gulkena River   stream, see Gulkana River.

GULL ISLAND   island, 1.3 km. (0.8 mi.) long, in Icy Bay 3.2 km. (2 mi.) NNE of Moraine Island; T 23 S, R 24 E, Copper River Mer.; 59°57'15" N, 141°21'30" W. Not: Bird Island, Egg Island, Esker Island, Fort Island, Seagull Island. BGN 8001.

GULL ISLAND   island, 0.16 km. (0.1 mi.) across, in Port Chester 1.6 km. (1 mi.) NW of Metlakatla; T 78 S, R 92 E, Copper River Mer.; 55°08'28" N, 131°35'35" W. Not: Crow Island. BGN 7903.

GULL LAKE   lake, low wetland, 2.4 km. (1.5 mi.) across, 2.9 km. (1.8 mi.) NW of Swan Lake and 11.3 km. (7 mi.) SE of Palmer; Matanuska-Susitna Borough; secs. 20, 21, 28, 29, and 30, T 17 N, R 3 E, Seward Mer.; 61°32'30" N, 148°56'45" W. BGN 8002.

Gun Creek   stream, see Gunn Creek.

GUNN CREEK   stream, 13 mi. long, heads at 63°13'10"N, 145°21'30" W, flows SW to Summit Lake 9 mi. N of Paxson; 63°09'55" N, 145°32'35" W. Not: Gun Creek. BGN 1969.

Guthna Creek   stream, see Boulder Creek.
Guthna Creek   stream, see Fish Creek.

HAL WAUGH, MOUNT	mountain, highest elevation 1,425 m. (4,678 ft.), bound on the E by the Iniakuk River, on the W by Tobuk Creek, and on the SW by Iniakuk Lake; named for Harold (Hal) Waugh (died 1973), guide and sportsman who owned property on the shore of nearby Iniakuk Lake; 67°11'25" N, 153°13'30" W. BGN 7401.
Haley Rock	rocks, see Haley Rocks.
HALEY ROCKS	rocks, along S shore of Fish Bay, at NW end of Baranof Island; named in 1896 by Commander Edwin King Moore, U.S. Navy, during hydrographic surveys in the area; 57°22'38" N, 135°37'47" W. Not: Haley Rock. BGN 8501.
Halfway Point	point of land, see Polovina Point.
HAND TROLLERS COVE	cove 1 mi. long, on the W side of Shelter Island, in the Saginaw Channel 20 mi. NW of Juneau; 58°26'50" N, 134°53'50" W. Not: Hand Troller's Cove, Shelter Cove. BGN 1968.
Hand Troller's Cove	cove, see Hand Trollers Cove.
HANKINSON PENINSULA	peninsula, 4 mi. long, between Dixon Harbor and Torch Bay 47 mi. SE of Mount Fairweather; named for Commander Ray L. Hankinson, U.S. Coast Guard (1879-1966), Inspector of Lighthouses for Alaska (1912-1913) who was responsible for the installation of acetylene lamps as aids to navigation; 58°20'00" N, 136°49'45" W. BGN 1968.
Hanus Island	island, see Hanus Islet.
HANUS ISLET	island, 0.16 km. (0.1 mi.) across, in the Necker Islands, at E point of entrance to Symonds Bay off N coast of Biorka Island 34 km. (15 mi.) SW of Sitka; named in 1879 by Lt. F. M. Symonds, USN, for Master (later Commander) Gustavus Charles Hanus (1846-1931), USN, who, with Lt. Symonds, surveyed this area in 1879; 56°51'55" N, 135°30'15" W. Not: Hanus Island. BGN 7801.

HARLEY CREEK	stream, 3 mi. long, on Chichagof Island, heads at 57°48'20" N, 135°07'00" W, flows E, then S, to Tenakee Inlet 5 mi. E of Tenakee Springs; 57°47'12" N, 135°05'20" W. BGN 1969.
HARP MOUNTAIN	mountain, elevation 5,001 ft., 2.7 mi. N of Eagle Lake and 16 mi. E. of Anchorage; 61°13'25" N, 149°23'30" W. BGN 1969.
HARRIS BAY	bay, 8 km. (5 mi.) long, on the S coast of Kenai Peninsula, extends S from Northwestern Fiord to the Gulf of Alaska W of Granite Island; 59°42'00" N, 149°53'00" W; 1910 description revised. BGN 8003.
Harris Bay	fiord, see Northwestern Fiord.
Healey Fork	village, see Healy.
HEALY	village, on the Nenana River, NW of the mouth of Healy Creek and 78 mi. SSW of Fairbanks; 63°51'25" N, 148°57'58" W. Not: Dry Creek, Healy Fork, Healey Fork. 1965. BGN 1968.
HEIDI ROCK	island, 0.32 km. (0.2 mi.) across, in Freshwater Bay, 3.7 km. (2.3 mi.) E of the Redcliff Islands and 16.9 km. (10.5 mi.) NE of Tenakee Springs; named in 1979 by NOS for the hydrographic control marker located on the island; 58°53'06" N, 135°01'24" W. BGN 8103.
HENRY EAKIN, MOUNT	mountain, elevation 4,827 ft., in the Ray Mountains 17 mi. W. of Mount Tozi and 42 mi. NNE of Tanana; named for Henry M. Eakin, geologist, who explored the Ray Mountains area in 1913; sec. 4, T 11 N, R 19 W, Fairbanks Mer.; 65°43'13" N, 151°31'00" W. BGN 7302.
HENRY'S ARM	cove, 0.32 km. (0.2 mi.) wide and 1.9 km. (1.2 mi.) long, on Admiralty Island, in Pybus Bay 80 km. (50 mi.) NE of Sitka; secs. 24 and 25, T 52 S, R 70 E, Copper River Mer.; 57°20'30" N, 134°06'35" W. BGN 7902.

HERNING LAKE   lake, 1.4 mi. long and 0.3 mi. wide; one of the Meadow Lakes in the Matanuska Valley 1.6 mi. NW of Pittman; named for Orville George Herning (died 1947), who came to Alaska in 1898 and was long associated with mining and business in this area; 61°36'45" N, 149°40'00" W. BGN 1969.

HESPERUS, MOUNT   mountain, elevation 9,828 ft., in Revelation Mountains 16 mi. NW of Mount Mausolus; 61°48'15' N, 154°08'38" W. Not: North Buttress. BGN 1968.

HIDDEN LAKE   lake, 2.1 km. (1.3 mi.) across, 53 km. (33 mi.) ESE of Delta Junction; secs. 16, 18, 19 20, and 25, T 11 S, R 16 E, Fairbanks Mer.; 63°57'00" N, 144°39'45" W. BGN 7702.

HIDEOUT HILL   hill, elevation 2,890 ft., 1.6 mi. N of Hidden Lake and 1.2 mi. W of Jean Lake, 29 mi. E of Soldotna; 60°30'26" N, 150°12'45" W. BGN 1969.

Hiko-Bukta Bay   bay, see Koyuktolik Bay.

HISLOP, MOUNT   peak, elevation 7,164 ft., in the Coast Mountains, on the Alaska-Canada boundary 3 mi. W of Mount Poletica; named for John Hislop, engineer in charge of construction of the White Pass and Yukon Railroad; sec. 36, T 31 S, and sec. 1, T 32 S, R 64 E, Copper River Mer.; 59°07'53" N, 134°33'55" W. Not: Boundary Peak 103. BGN 1972.

HOLLAND CREEK   stream, 1.3 km. (0.8 mi.) long, heads at 60°24'07" N, 144°10'08" W, flows SSW to Carbon Creek 3.2 km. (2 mi.) W of Kushtaka Lake; sec. 21, T 17 S, R 7 E, Copper River Mer.; 60°23'30" N, 144°10'38" W. BGN 7504.

HOLLIS   locality, ferry boat landing on Prince of Wales Island, 31 km. (19 mi.) E of Craig; sec. 4, T 74 S, R 84 E, Copper River Mer.; 55°28'53" N, 132°39'00" W. BGN 7603.

HOLMES, MOUNT	peak, elevation 7,720 ft., in the Wrangell Mountains, 2.2 mi. NW of Andrus Peak and 5 mi. W of Pyramid Peak; 61°18'21" N, 142°29'07" W. BGN 1967.
HOOK CREEK	stream, 8.4 km. (5.2 mi.) long, heads at 57°38'44" N, 135°07'03" W, flows NW to the Kadashan River 4 km. (2.5 mi.) SE of Kadashan Bay and 70 km. (44 mi.) N of Sitka; Sitka Borough; sec. 27, T 48 S, R 63 E, Copper River Mer.; 57°40'33" N, 135°11'38" W. BGN 8301.
Hook Creek	stream, see Tonalite Creek.
HUB ROCK	rock, in Port Chester 1.9 km. (1.2 mi.) NE of Metlakatla; T 78 S, R 92 E, Copper River Mer.; 55°08'20" N, 131°33'00" W. Not: Devils Rock. BGN 7903.
HUE CREEK	stream, 4 km. (2.5 mi.) long, heads at 69°33'00" N, 145°50'00" W, flows N to Ignek Creek 12.9 km. (8 mi.) NE of Mount Copleston; named for the varied colored rock through which the stream flows; sec. 30, T 3 N, R 26 E, Umiat Mer.; 69°34'50" N, 145°49'35" W. BGN 7501.
Huiakan River	stream, see Eulachon River.
Hulakan River	stream, see Eulachon River.
Hulakin River	stream, see Eulachon River.
Hulakon River	stream, see Eulachon River.
Humpback Point	point of land, see Kooisk Point.
HURDYGURDY MOUNTAIN	mountain, elevation 5,965 ft., 1.5 mi. NE of Eagle Lake and 19 mi. ESE of Anchorage; 61°11'22" N. 149°18'45" W. BGN 1969.
Huxley Peak	peak, see Huxley, Mount.
HUXLEY, MOUNT	peak, elevation 12,216 ft., in Saint Elias Mountains 2.4 mi. NW of The Hump and 48 mi. NE of Cape Yakataga; 60°19'40" N, 141°09'30" W. Not: Huxley Peak (former decision). BGN 1917. BGN 1968.

ICY BAY	bay, 17.7 km. (11 mi.) long, on the E coast of Kenai Peninsula, trends NE from Tiger Glacier to open out 8 km. (5 mi.) W of Chenega; Tps. 1 and 2 N, Rgs. 6 and 7 E, Seward Mer.; 60°17'00" N, 148°12'30" W (NE end), 60°10'50" N, 148°26'40" W (SW end); 1978 description revised. Not: Icy Fiord. BGN 7903.
Icy Fiord	bay, see Icy Bay.
Icy Peak	mountain, see Calliope Mountain.
IGILATVIK CREEK	stream, 35 km. (22 mi.) long, heads at 69°29'55" N, 143°34'55" W, flows N to the Jago River 56 km. (35 mi.) N of Mount Hubley; sec. 20, T 5 N, R 34 E, Umiat Mer.; 69°46'09" N, 143°26'45" W. BGN 7402.
Igna-look	locality, see Inalik.
Ignaluk	locality, see Inalik.
Il-luit-kuk	island, see Doctor Island.
INALIK	locality, on W coast of Little Diomede Island in Bering Strait 2.4 km. (1.5 mi.) SW of Diomede; 65°45'40" N, 168°56'00" W. Variants: Diomede, Inalit, Igna-look, Ignaluk. BGN 7603.
INDEPENDENCE CREEK	stream, 8.9 km. (5.5 mi.) long, heads 8.9 km. (5.5 mi.) W of Takotna at 62°58'42" N, 156°15'10" W, flows N to Ready Bullion Creek 16.9 km. (10.5 mi.) SE of Ophir; sec. 30, T 28 S, R 14 E, Kateel River Mer.; 63°02'25" N, 156°16'38" W. BGN 8402.
Independence Creek	stream, see Ready Bullion Creek.
INDIAN POINT	point of land, on E shore of Frederick Sound at N entrance to Le Conte Bay 27 km. (17 mi.) SE of Petersburg; secs. 17 and 20, T 59 S, R 82 E, Copper River Mer.; 56°45'00" N, 132°31'30" W. BGN 7702.
Inner Point Sophia	point of land, see Cannery Point.

INSTITUTE PEAK	peak, elevation over 8,000 ft., between Gulkana and West Gulkana Glaciers 5 mi. WNW of Icefall Peak; 63°17'35" N, 145°29'54" W. BGN 1969.
INUALURAK MOUNTAIN	mountain, elevation 6,770 ft., in the Brooks Range 13 mi. NW of the village of Anaktuvuk Pass; named for Hugo Inualurak, an Eskimo hunter who, at his death in 1967, was the head of a patrilineal descent group; 68°12'30" N, 152°13'00" W. BGN 1969.
INUPIAT MOUNTAIN	mountain, elevation 6,600 ft., in the Brooks Range, 22 mi. W of the village of Anaktuvuk Pass; named for the Inupiat Eskimo people who inhabit the area; 68°09'00" N, 152°35'00" W. 1969 decision VACATED. BGN 1970.
IRON DOOR, THE	point of land, on the W shore of Resurrection Peninsula extending S between Humpy Cove and Resurrection Bay, 11.3 km. (7 mi.) NNW of Cape Resurrection; Kenai Peninsula Borough; sec. 29, T 2 S, R 1 E, Seward Mer.; 59°58'21" N, 149°19'18" W. BGN 8003.
Iron Mountain	mountain, see Benson Mount.
IRVIN THOMPSON MOUNTAIN	mountain, elevation 715 m. (2,344 ft.), on Gravina Island 5.6 km. (3.5 mi.) W of Ketchikan; named for Irvin Thompson (1918-1941), who was probably the first Alaskan to die in World War II; secs. 19 and 20, T 75 S, R 90 E, Copper River Mer.; 55°21'06" N, 131°46'35" W. BGN 7504.
ISLAND LAKE	lake, 1.5 km. (0.9 mi.) long, one of the Meadow Lakes located S of Totuk Lake 11 km. (6.8 mi.) NW of Wasilla; Matanuska-Susitna Borough; secs. 22 and 27, T 18 N, R 2 W, Seward Mer.; 61°37'45" N, 149°37'00" W. BGN 8002.
ITIGAKNIT LAKE	lake, 1.5 mi. long, 5 mi. SE of Itigaknit Mountain; secs. 1 and 12, T 9 S, R 10 E, and sec. 6, T 9 S, R 11 E, Umiat Mer.; 68°41'10" N, 149°40'30" W. Not: Toolik Lake. BGN 1972.

IZMAYLOV ISLAND island, 0.32 km. (0.2 mi.) long, in Latouoche Passage between Elrington and Latouche Islands 80 km. (50 mi.) ESE of Seward; named for G. A. Izmaylov (Izmailov), who served as co-commander of the Russian vessel Three Saints and in 1788 with Dmitrii Ivanovich Bocharoav explored the shore of the Gulf of Alaska from the Kenai Peninsula to Lituya Bay; secs. 12 and 13, T 2 S, R 8 E, Seward Mer.; 60°00'35" N, 147°59'15" W. BGN 8002.

JADE HARBOR	cove, 0.64 km. (0.4 mi.) across, on shore of Heather Bay 4.8 km. (3 mi.) NE of Elf Point and 17.2 km. (10.7 mi. NW of Ellamar; sec. 27, T 10 S, R 10 W, Copper River Mer.; 60°58'15" N, 146°58'30" W. BGN 8003.
JADE LAKE	lake, 0.3 mi. long, 6 mi. NW of Knik and 21 mi. N of Anchorage; secs. 31 and 32, T 17 N, R 3 W, Seward Mer.; 61°31'30" N, 149°52'05" W. BGN 1971.
JAMES DALTON MOUNTAIN	mountain, elevation 2,164 m. (7,100 ft.), in the Endicott Mountains 26 km. (16.5 mi.) SE of Itkillik Lake; named for James Dalton (1913-1977), pioneer Alaskan who was active in many of the early petroleum exploration activities and who was instrumental in the States selection of land in the Prudhoe Bay area where massive quantities of oil and gas were later found; sec. 26, T 14 S, R 11 E, Umiat Mer.; 68°12'00" N, 149°31'40" W. BGN 7803.
JAW POINT	point of land, in Glacier Bay National Monument along the east shore of Johns Hopkins Inlet, 29 km. (18 mi.) E of Mount Fairweather; sec. 23, T 34 S, R 50 E, Copper River Mer.; 58°54'13" N, 137°00'55" W. BGN 8103.
JEANIE CREEK	stream, 3 mi. long, on Montague Island, heads at 59°52'15" N, 147°39'20" W, flows SE ot Jeanie Cove 2.8 mi. NW of Jeanie Point; 59°51'10" N, 147°36'45" W. BGN 1967.
JESSE CREEK	stream, 7.2 km. (4.5 mi.) long, heads at 63°41'37" N, 160°42'10" W, flows NW to Norton Sound between Summer Camp and Coal Mine Creeks 13.7 km. (8.5 mi.) S of Unalakleet; sec. 22, T 20 S, R 11 W, Kateel River Mer.; 63°44'50" N, 160°47'15" W. Not: Cascade Creek, Glacier Creek. BGN 8103.
Jimmy Orr Creek	stream, see Painter Creek.
John Island	island, see Road Island.

Johnson Pass • pass, see Turnagain Pass.

JOHNSON ROCK • rock, submerged, off the S end of Battery Point in Chilkoot Inlet 5.6 km. (3.5 mi.) SE of Haines; named for Harold A. Johnson (1923-1975), sea captain who owned and operated a cannery tender out of Haines and who was Master of the M/V *Matanuska* for 11 years; 59°12'24" N, 135°21'36" W. BGN 7902.

JOHNSON SLOUGH • cove, 0.64 km. (0.4 mi.) across, 3.2 km. (2 mi.) NW of Port Graham and 11 km. (6.8 mi.) SW of Seldovia; Kenai Peninsula Borough; secs. 19, 20, 29, and 30, T 9 S, R 15 W, Seward Mer.; 59°22'30" N, 151°52'30" W; 1978 decision revised. Not: Celenie Lake, Selenie Lagoon (BGN 1978). BGN 8203.

JOHNSONS SLOUGH • water passage, 0.8 km. (0.5 mi.) long, an extension of Kunayosh Creek in the mud flats at its mouth, extends SSE from the mouth of Kunayosh Creek to the Situk River 0.48 (0.3 mi.) NE of Situk; 59°26'45" N, 139°33'10" W (NW end) 59°26'15" N, 139°33'00" W (SE end); 1978 decision revised. Not: Kunayosh Creek. BGN 8003.

JONATHAN WARD, MOUNT • peak, elevation 1,438 m. (4,719 ft.), 9.7 km. (6 mi.) SSW of Klukwan; named for Jonathan F. Ward (1951-1975), who lost his life working for the Alaska Department of Fish and Game; sec. 34, T 29 S, R 56 E, Copper River Mer.; 59°19'08" N, 135°56'58" W. BGN 7504.

JONES CREEK • stream, 0.4 mi. long, in the Aleutian Islands, heads in Jones Lake on Amchitka Island, flows ENE to Constantine Harbor; named for the lake of the same name; 51°24'12" N, 179°16'32" E. BGN 1969.

JOSHUA GREEN PEAK   peak, elevation 2,175 m. (7,135 ft.), in the Wrangell Mountains 29km. (18 mi.) ESE of McCarthy; named for Joshua Green (1869-1975), philanthropist, who through his financial backing of miners was instrumental in mineral development in the Dan Creek area; sec. 5, T 6 S, R 17 E, Copper River Mer.; 61°22'18" N, 142°24'05" W. BGN 7504.

JOSHUA GREEN RIVER   stream, 7.2 km. (4.5 mi.) long, heads at 55°20'20" N, 162°28'00" W, flows N for 3.2 km. (2 mi.) then NW to Moffet Lagoon 27 km. (17 mi.) NE of the village of Cold Bay; T 55 S, R 87 W, Seward Mer.; 55°23'30" N, 162°29'10" W. BGN 8402.

JUMA REEF   reef, 1.5 km. (0.9 mi.) long, in Kamishak Bay 0.81 km. (0.5 mi.) N of Nordyke Island; 59°11'30" N, 154°04'20" W. BGN 7504.

JUNE BIFFLE LAKE   lake, 0.81 km. (0.5 mi.) across, in the Matanuska Valley along course of Sawmill Creek 2.4 km. (1.5 mi.) E of Bonnie Lake and 51 km. (32 mi.) NE of Palmer; named for June Biffle, who homesteaded here with her husband, Roy; sec. 19, T 20 N, R 7 E, Seward Mer.; 61°48'45" N, 148°15'10" W. Not: Upper Bonnie Lake. BGN 7704.

KACHEMAK SILO   populated place, on NW shore of Kachemak Bay along the lower course of Fox Creek, 32 km. (20 mi.) E of Nikolaevsk and 32 km. (20 mi.) NE of Homer; settled in late 1970s by Russian immigrants from nearby Nikolaevsk; the name means "Kachemak Settlement"; secs. 30 and 31, T 4 S, R 10 W, Seward Mer.; 59°48'00" N, 151°03'30" W. BGN 8103.

KAGEET POINT   point of land, on E side of Icy Bay at S entrance to Taan Fiord 21 km. (13 mi.) NNE of Point Riou; 60°03'35" N, 141°19'30" W. BGN 7303.

KALHABUK MOUNTAIN   mountain, elevation 1,522 m. (4,995 ft.), 6.1 km. (3.8 mi.) W of Wiseman and 7.2 km. (4.5 mi.) E of Bluecloud Mountain; named for Florence Jonas (1897-1979) whose Eskimo name was "Kalhabuk", who at the time of her death had lived in Wiseman longer than any other person; secs. 21 and 28, T 30 N, R 12 W, Fairbanks Mer.; 67°24'16" N, 150°14'45" W. BGN 8004.

Kalifonski   locality, see Kalifornsky.

Kalifonsky   locality, see Kalifornsky.

Kalifonsky Beach   beach, see Kalifornsky Beach.

KALIFORNSKY   locality, along Cook Inlet, 16 km. (10 mi.) S of Kenai; a name given to a Dena'ina (Tanaina) Indian who worked at the Fort Ross colony in California between 1812 and the 1820's; Kenai Peninsula Borough; 60°25'00" N, 151°17'15" W. Not: Kalifonski, Kalifonsky (BGN 1916). BGN 8504.

KALIFORNSKY BEACH   beach, 14.5 km. (9 mi.) long, along Cook Inlet, extends N from Kalifornsky to the Kenai River S of Kenai; Kenai Peninsula Borough; 60°28'30" N, 151°16'45" W. Not: Kalifonsky Beach. BGN 8504.

KALMBACH LAKE	lake, 1.3 km. (0.8 mi.) long, 7.2 km. (4.5 mi.) NW of Wasilla; named for the family of George F. Kalmbach, who homesteaded in the area in 1956; secs. 35 and 36; T 18 N, R 2 W, Seward Mer.; 61°36'30" N, 149°34'10" W. Variant: Kalmback Lake. BGN 7501.
Kalmback Lake	lake, see Kalmbach Lake.
KASILOF	village, on Kenai Peninsula, 2.3 mi. SE of Cohoe; 60°20'10" N, 151°16'00" W. Not: Kassilow, Kussilof, Kussilow. 1945. BGN 1969.
KASNYKU CREEK	stream, 0.8 mi. long, on Baranof Island, heads at Kasnyku Lake, flows ENE to Waterfall Cove 21 mi. NE of Sitka; 57°11'30" N, 134°50'00" W. Not: Kasnyku Lake Outlet. BGN 1968.
Kasnyku Lake Outlet	stream see Kasnyku Creek.
Kassilow	village, see Kasilof.
KATMAI ROCK	rock, in Katmai National Monument, in Katmai Bay, Shelikof Strait, 3.2 km. (2 mi.) SE of Katmai Village site and 4 km. (2.5 mi.) SW of Mount Pedmar; 58°00'21" N, 154°51'04" W. BGN 8203.
Kauichungak Creek	stream, see Koweejoongak River.
Kekau Islets	islands, see Keku Islands.
KEKU ISLANDS	islands, largest 2.6 km. (1.6 mi.) long, at N end of Keku Strait 10 km. (6.2 mi.) SW of Kake; 56°57°28" N, 134°08'45" W (NW end), 56°53'53" N, 133°57'30" W (SE end). Variants: Kekau Islets, Keku Islets, Kiku Islets. BGN 7702.
Keku Islets	islands, see Keku Islands.
Kennedy Creek	stream, see Midnight Creek.
Ketavie Point	point of land, see Kitovi Point.
Kiawak Inlet	water passage, see Klawock Inlet.

KICHATNA SPIRE	peak, elevation 8,985 ft., one of the Cathedral Spires in the Kichatna Mountains, 1.5 mi. NW of Gurney Peak; 62°25'20" N, 152°43'15" W. BGN 1967.
KICHYATT POINT	point of land, on W side of Icy Bay 16 km. (10 mi.) NNE of Point Riou; exposed by recent retreat of Guyot Glacier; 60°01'38" N, 141°22'00" W. BGN 7303.
KIDAZQENI GLACIER	glacier, 7.2 km. (4.5 mi.) long, heads on the SE slope of Mount Spurr, trends SE towards the Chakachatna River 54 km. (34 mi.) WNW of Tyonek; kidazqeni is the anglicized spelling of the Dena'ina name for Mount Spurr meaning "the one that is burning inside"; Kenai Peninsula Bor.; Tps. 13 and 14 N, Rgs. 16 and 17 W, Seward Mer.; 61°13'35" N, 152°07'15" W (SE end), 61°17'00" N, 152°13'00" W (NW end). BGN 8402.
Kiku Islets	islands, see Keku Islands.
KILLESTOK CREEK	stream, 8.1 km. (5 mi.) long, heads at 65°25'45" N, 166°37'20" W, flows SE to the California River 18 km. (11 mi.) NE of Point Spencer; Inupik Eskimo word meaning "fossil-shell creek"; 65°23'50" N, 166°35'30" W. BGN 7501.
KILOKAK ROCKS	rocks, 3.8 km. (2.4 mi.) ESE of Cape Kilokak; 57°09'25" N, 156°16'40" W. Variant: Rochers Kilikak. BGN 7504.
Kinarak Creek	stream, see Kinaruk River.
Kinaruk Creek	stream, see Kinaruk River.
KINARUK RIVER	stream, 35 km. (22 mi.) long, heads at 60°35'55" N, 163°52'00" W, flows W to Kolavinerak River 10.5 km. (6.5 mi.) NE of Emperor Island; sec. 23, T 6 N, R 86 W, Seward Mer.; 60°35'31" N, 164°19'45" W. Variants: Amadens Creek, Amadeus Creek, Kinarak Creek, Kinaruk Creek. BGN 7501.
KING COVE HARBOR	cove, 0.16 km. (0.1 mi.) across, at S end of King Cove Lagoon 0.48 km. (0.3 mi.) W of King Cove village; 55°03'33" N, 162°19'30" W. BGN 7504.

KING GEORGE BAY	cove, 0.48 km. (0.3 mi.) across and 1 km. (0.7 mi.) long, on NW coast of Etolin Island 3.2 km. (2 mi.) S of entrance from Chichagof Pass into Stikine Strait 21 km. (13 mi.) SSW of Wrangell; secs. 13 and 24, T 64 S, R 82 E and secs. 18 and 19, T 64 S, R 83 E, Copper River Mer.; 56°19'00" N, 132°32'42" W. BGN 8102.
King Lake	lake, see Kings, Lake.
KINGS LAKE	lake, 1.1 km. (0.7 mi.) long, separated from Anderson Lake on the E by a narrow neck of land, 5.6 km. (3.5 mi.) NE of Wasilla; Matanuska-Susitna Borough; sec. 30, T 18 N, R 1 E, and sec. 25, T 18 N, R 1 W, Seward Mer.; 61°37'05" N, 149°21'25" W; 1978 description revised. Not: Fishhook Lake, King Lake. BGN 7904.
Kings Lake	lake, see Anderson Lake.
Kiokluk Lake	lake, see Tevyaraq Lake.
Kirilof Cove	cove, see Cyril Cove.
KITOVI POINT	point of land, on the SE coast of Saint Paul Island in the Pribilof Islands 1.6 km. (1 mi.) NE of the village of Saint Paul; name derived from Russian name Mys Kitovyy, meaning "whale cape", and reported by H. W. Elliott in 1881 as "Ketavie" because a "right whale was stranded here in 1849"; 57°07'30" N, 170°15'20" W; 1978 decision revised. Not: Ketavie Point, Whale Point (BGN 1978), Mys Kitovyy. BGN 8103.
Klawack Inlet	water passage, see Klawock Inlet.
Klawack Strait	water passage, see Klawock Inlet.
Klawak Creek	stream, see Klawock River.
Klawak Harbor	harbor, see Klawock Harbor.
Klawak Inlet	water passage, see Klawock Inlet.

Klawak Island	island, see Klawock Island.
Klawak Lake	lake, see Klawock Lake.
Klawak Passage	water passage, see Klawock Inlet.
Klawak Reef	reef, see Klawock Reef.
Klawak River	stream, see Klawock River.
Klawak Stream	stream, see Klawock River.
KLAWOCK HARBOR	harbor, 1 mi. long, on W coast of Prince of Wales Island between Klawock and Klawock Island; 55°33' N, 133°06' W. Not: Klawak Harbor. BGN 1968.
KLAWOCK INLET	water passage, 9 mi. long, in the Alexander Archipelago between Fish Egg and Wadleigh Islands, on the W, and Prince of Wales Island, on the E, N of Craig; 55°32' N, 133°07' W. Not Kiawak Inlet, Klawack Inlet, Klawack Strait, Klawak Inlet, Klawak Passage, Klawok Inlet, Kliavakhan Inlet, Tlevakh Inlet, Tlevak Inlet, Tlevakkhyn Bay, Zaliv Tlevakkhan. BGN 1968.
KLAWOCK ISLAND	island, 1 mi. long, on W coast of Prince of Wales Island, between Klawock Harbor and Klawock Inlet, 0.2 mi. W of Klawock; 55°33'00" N, 133°06'20" W. Not: Klawak Island, La Galera. BGN 1968.
KLAWOCK LAKE	lake, 7 mi. long, on W coast of Prince of Wales Island 2 mi. E of Klawock; 55°31' N, 132°39' W. Not: Klawak Lake. BGN 1968.
KLAWOCK REEF	reef, 0.7 mi. long, on W coast of Prince of Wales Island, N of Fish Egg Island between Klawock Inlet and San Alberto Bay; 55°30'45" N, 133°10'30" W. Not: Klawak Reef. BGN 1968.
KLAWOCK RIVER	stream, 2.3 mi. long, on W coast of Prince of Wales Island, heads in Klawock Lake, flows W to Klawock Harbor S of Klawock; 55°32'57" N, 133°05'45" W. Not: Klawak Creek, Klawak River, Klawak Stream. BGN 1968.

Klawok Inlet					water passage, see Klawock Inlet.

Kliavakhan Inlet				water passage, see Klawock Inlet.

KNIK ARM SHOAL				shoal, 4 km. (2.5 mi.) W of Point Woronzof, in Knik Arm 8.9 km. (5.5 mi.) W of Anchorage; 61°12'17" N, 150°05'17" W. BGN 7504.

KNOB CREEK					stream, 3.5 km. (2.2 mi.) long, heads at 61°45'35" N, 148°52'01" W, flows SSW to Eska Creek 0.8 km. (0.5 mi.) S of Eska and 19.3 km. (12 mi.) NE of Palmer; sec. 15, T 19 N, R 3 E, Seward Mer.; 61°43'55" N, 148°54'15" W; 1946 description revised. BGN 7801.

Knob Creek					stream, see Eska Creek.

KOKA ISLAND PASSAGE			water passage, 1.9 km. (1.2 mi.) long, connects Redoubt Bay with Sitka Sound 13.7 km. (8.5 mi.) S of Sitka; 56°55'15" N, 135°23'15" W (N end), 56°54'15" N, 135°23'15" W (S end). BGN 7904.

KOOISK POINT				point of land, on SE shore of Yakutat Bay 13.7 km. (8.5 mi.) NE of Yakutat; sec. 24, T 26 S, R 34 E, Copper River Mer.; 59°38'33" N, 139°35'00" W. Variant: Humpback Point. BGN 7702.

KOOK CREEK					stream, 7.5 mi. long, on Chichagof Island, heads at 57°37'10" N, 135°05'05" W, flows NE through Kook Lake to Basket Bay, 46 mi. NNE of Sitka; 57°40'05" N, 134°56'05" W. BGN 1968.

KOWEEJOONGAK RIVER			stream, 16.1 km. (10 mi.) long, on Nunivak Island, heads at 60°11'07" N, 166°04'35" W, flows N to Etolin Strait 14.5 km. (9 mi.) SSE of Cape Etolin; Eskimo name reported by NOS in 1949; sec. 25, T 3 N, R 97 W, Seward Mer.; 60°19'15" N, 166°03'45" W. Not: Kauichungak Creek, Koweejoougak River. BGN 8203.

Koweejoougak River			stream, see Koweejoongak River.

KOYUKTOLIK BAY	bay, 3.2 km. (2 mi.) across, on the E shore of Cook Inlet at SW tip of the Kenai Peninsula 12.9 km. (8 mi.) SW of Port Graham; Kenai Peninsula Borough; T 11 S, Rgs. 15 and 16 W, Seward Mer.; 59°14'30" N, 151°56'00" W; 1908 description revised. Not: Dogfish Bay, Dog Salmon Bay, Hiko-Bukta Bay. BGN 8301.
KRAUSE, MOUNT	mountain, elevation over 7,000 ft., in Takhinsha Mountains, 5.5 mi. NNE of Sitth-gha-ee Peak and 16 mi. WSW of Haines; named for the brothers Arthur and Aurel Krause, who made ethnographic and geographic studies in this area in 1881-82; 59°11'00" N, 135°53'35" W. BGN 1967.
KUGEL CREEK	stream, 5 mi. long, on Prince of Wales Island, heads at 55°06'50" N, 132°15'40" W, flows S to unnamed arm of Dickman Bay 32 mi. SW of Ketchikan; 55°02'45" N, 132°15'08" W. BGN 1969.
KUGEL LAKE	lake, 1.6 mi. long, on Prince of Wales Island, 30 mi. SW of Ketchikan; 55°04'00" N, 132°14'30" W. BGN 1969.
Kulkana River	stream, see Gulkana River.
KUNAYOSH CREEK	stream, 14.5 km. (9 mi.) long, heads at 59°33'00" N, 139°28'00" W, flows SW to a point where it continues as Johnsons Slough 1 km. (0.6 mi.) N of Situk; 59°26'45" N, 139°33'10" W; 1978 description revised. BGN 8003.
Kunayosh Creek	water passage, see Johnsons Slough.
KURUPA HILLS	hills, highest elevation over 4,200 ft., in a group trending NW-SE 5 mi., on the N side of the Brooks Range, 2 mi. W of Kurupa Lake and 53 mi. ENE of Howard Pass; 68°22' N, 154°48' W. 1966. BGN 1967.
Kusalvak	island, see Kusilvak.

KUSHTAKA MOUNTAIN	mountain, highest elevation 742 m. (2,435 ft.), between Lake Charlotte and Shepherd Creek on the W and Kushtaka Glacier and Lake on the E; Tps. 16 and 17 S, R 7 E, Copper River Mer.; 60°27'15" N, 144°05'30" W (NE end), 60°22'00" N, 144°12'30" W (SW end). BGN 7504.
KUSILVAK	island, Yukon Delta, Bering Sea. Not Kusalvak. VACATED. 1860. BGN 1966.
Kussilof	village, see Kasilof.
Kussilow	village, see Kasilof.

L V RAY PEAK	peak, elevation 1,475 m. (4,840 ft.), in the Kenai Mountains, between Crescent and Upper Trail Lakes 40 km. (25 mi.) N of Seward; named for L. V. Ray (1877-1946), attorney and president of the first Alaska Senate in 1913; sec. 34, T 5 N, R 1 W, Seward Mer.; 60°29'00" N, 149°25'20" W. BGN 7802.
La Galera	island, see Klawock Island.
LADYSLIPPER LAKE	lake,, 1.1 km. (0.7 mi.) long, 20.9 km. (13 mi.) N of Susitna; secs. 16 and 21, T 19 N, R 7 W, Seward Mer.; 61°44'00" N, 150°33'15" W. BGN 7503.
Lake Edes	lake, see Edes Lake.
Lake Edes	lake, see Summit Lake.
Lake Nancy	lake, see Nancy Lake.
Lake Noluck	lake, see Nullaq Lake.
Lake Noluk	lake, see Nullaq Lake.
LAKESIDE	roadhouse, north of Seward, on Alaska Northern Railroad; VACATED. 1966. BGN 1966.
LAMB GLACIER	glacier, 2 mi. long, heads at 61°04'00" N, 141°15'30" W, trends SW to Ewe Glacier 5 mi. SSW of Mount Tittman; 61°02'50" N, 141°18'20" W. BGN 1967.
LANDSLIDE COVE	cove, 0.4 mi. wide, in the Aleutian Islands, along the N coast of Amchitka Island 0.5 mi. S of Low Bluff and 1.3 mi. SE of Chitka Cove; named for the landslide behind the cove; 51°34'20" N, 178°59'23" E. BGN 1969.
LANGILLE MOUNTAIN	mountain, elevation 4,297 ft., 3.2 mi. ENE of the village of Cooper Landing and 30 mi. NNW of Seward; named for William Alexander Langille, Alaska's first forester, who was instrumental in the creation of the Sitka and Old Kasaan National Monuments, Kenai National Moose Range, and the Kenai addition to Chugach National Forest; 60°30'45" N, 149°44'45" W. Not: Dall Mountain, Goat Mountain, Sheep Mountain. BGN 1972.

LARK MOUNTAIN	mountain, highest elevation over 5,700 ft., 2.7 mi. E of Upper Trail Lake and 3.7 mi. ENE of the village of Moose Pass; named for the horned lark (Eremophila alpestris), only lark found in Alaska and spotted on the slopes of this mountain; 60°30'42" N, 149°16'27" W. BGN 1971.
LAST CHANCE HARBOR	cove, 0.48 km. (0.3 mi.) wide and 2.4 km. (1.5 mi.) long, on the SE shore of Admiralty Island 100 km. (62 mi.) NE of Sitka; secs 4, 5 and 9, T 51 S, R 72 E, Copper River Mer.; 57°28'00" N, 133°52'00" W. BGN 7902.
LAVA MOUNTAIN	mountain, elevation 6,620 ft., in the Talkeetna Mountains 9 mi. NE of Sutton; named for the lava flows located on the N and NW slopes; 61°49'35" N, 148°45'48" W. BGN 1972.
LEAF LAKE	lake, 0.32 km. (0.2 mi.) long, just NE of Swan Lake and 14.5 km. (9 mi.) SE of Palmer; Matanuska-Susitna Borough; sec. 27, T 17 N, R 3 E, Seward Mer.; 61°32'15" N, 148°53'05" W. BGN 8002.
LEANNE, LAKE	lake, 0.6 mi. long, on Kodiak Island, 2 mi. SW of the S end of Kizhuyak Bay and 19 mi. SW of Kodiak; 57°42'15" N, 152°45'35" W. BGN 1967.
LEDYARD BAY	bight, 160 km. (100 mi.) long, between Point Lay and Cape Lisburne; named for John Ledyard (1751-1789), American adventurer who traveled with Captain James Cook through this bay in 1778; 69°45'00" N, 163°04'00" W (N end), 68°53'00" N, 166°13'00" W (S end). BGN 7504.
LEE ROCK	rock, in Clarence Strait 0.48 km. (0.3 mi.) NW of Three Islands and 4.5 km. (2.8 mi.) SSE of Meyers Chuck; 55°42'15" N, 132°14'15" W. BGN 7501.

LEFFINGWELL FORK	stream, 45 km. (28 mi.) long, heads at 69°06'20" N, 142°38'10" W, flows NNW to Aichilik River 37 km. (23 mi.) NE of Mount Hubley; named for Ernest de Koven Leffingwell (1876-1971), polar explorer and geologist, who over a period of 9 years in the early 1900's explored and mapped the coastal area of northern Alaska; sec. 15, T 1 N, R 37 E, Umiat Mer.; 69°26'48" N, 143°00'00" W. BGN 7504.
LELAND, MOUNT	peak, elevation 7,810 ft., 6 mi. SW of Mount Canning; named for O. M. Leland, who led the International Boundary Commission party of 1907; sec. 22, T 31 S, R 63 E, Copper River Mer.; 59°10'13" N, 134°47'27" W. BGN 1972.
Lester River	stream, see Staney Creek.
Lime Peak	mountain, see Rocky Mountain.
LIMPET CREEK	stream, 2 mi. long, in the Aleutian Islands, heads at 51°32'00" N, 179°00'43" E, flows WSW to the Pacific Ocean on the S coast of Amchitka Island 2.7 mi. SE of Andesite Point; named for the limpets found on the coast; 51°31'35" N, 178°58'15" E. BGN 1969.
LION CREEK	stream, 3.2 km. (2 mi.) long, heads at 64°26'15" N, 155°36'43" W, flows S to Basin Creek 37 km. (23 mi.) S of Ruby; sec. 35, T 12 S, R 16 E, Kateel River Mer.; 64°24'33" N, 155°37'07" W; 1936 decision revised. Not: Swift Creek (former decision). BGN 7704.
LISBURNE PENINSULA	peninsula, extends W 100 km. (62 mi.) from a line between Cape Beaufort and Kivalina, into the Chukchi Sea; named for Cape Lisburne, located on the NW point of the peninsula; 68°30'00" N, 165°15'00" W. BGN 7402.
LITEN LAKE	lake, 0.97 km. (0.6 mi.) long, 6.1 km. (3.8 mi.) NW of Knik and 22.2 km. (13.8 mi.) SW of Wasilla; "liten" is the Norwegian word for "small"; sec. 9, T 16 N, R 3 W, Seward Mer.; 61°29'45" N, 149°48'45" W. Not: Faith Lake. BGN 7801.

LITTLE ALINCHAK BAY	bay, 4.8 km. (3 mi.) wide, on W shore of Shelikof Strait, SW section of Alinchak Bay 15.5 km. (9.6 mi.) SW of Mount Kubugakli and 58 km. (36 mi.) WNW of Karluk; T 28 S, R 37 W, Seward Mer.; 57°46'45" N, 155°18'00" W. BGN 8401.
LITTLE ALINCHAK CREEK	stream, 5.6 km. (3.5 mi.) long, heads at 57°48'48" N, 155°26'05" W, flows ESE to Little Alinchak Bay 17.7 km. (11 mi.) SW of Mount Kubugakli and 58 km. (36 mi.) WNW of Karluk; sec. 4, T 28 S, R 37 W, Seward Mer.; 57°47'30" N, 155°21'40" W. BGN 8401.
Little Bill Lake	lake, see Montana Lake.
LITTLE CAMPBELL LAKE	lake, 0.48 km. (0.3 mi.) long, 2.4 km. (1.5 mi.) E of Point Campbell and 8 km. (5 mi.) SW of Anchorage; sec. 5, T 12 N, R 4 W, Seward Mer.; 61°09'43" N, 150°01'20" W; 1978 decision revised. Not: Beercan Lake, Campbell Lake (BGN 1978). BGN 8002.
LITTLE MERGANSER LAKE	lake, 0.32 km. (0.2 mi.) long, on the Kenai Peninsula 22.5 km. (14 mi.) NNE of Sterling; named about 1963 by officials of the Kenai National Moose Range, probably for the American Merganser or Pond Shelldrake (Mergus americanus), a large freshwater duck which breeds in southern Alaska; Kenai Peninsula Borough; sec. 2, T 7 N, R 8 W, Seward Mer.; 60°43'48" N, 150°38'05" W. BGN 8504.
LITTLE MONTANA CREEK	stream, 3 mi. long, heads in Montana Lake at 62°08'21" N, 150°02'55" W, flows S to the Susitna River 15 mi. S of Talkeetna; 62°06'32" N, 150°04'15" W. Not: Slow Montana Creek. BGN 1969.
LITTLE NUGGET CREEK	stream, 1.5 mi. long, heads on Ester Dome at 64°54'10" N, 148°01'16" W, flows NE to Goldstream Creek 10 mi. NW of Fairbanks; 64°54'47" N, 147°59'55" W. Not: Little Sheep Creek (former decision). BGN 1939. BGN 1969.

Little Russina Mission — settlement, see Chuathbaluk.

Little Sheep Creek — stream, see Little Nugget Creek.

LITTLE TUTKA BAY — cove, 0.8 mi. long, on Kenai Peninsula, on S side of entrance to Tutka Bay, 0.7 mi. SE of the Herring Islands and 12 mi. SSE of Homer; 59°28'30" N, 151°29'20" W. BGN 1967.

LOBERG LAKE — lake, 700 ft. across, 1.5 mi. NW of Matanuska; named for Lauritz Konrad Moller Loberg, original owner of property surrounding the lake; sec. 15, T 17 N, R 1 E, Seward Mer.; 61°33'35" N, 149°15'30" W. BGN 1972.

LOHI CREEK — stream, 8 km. (5 mi.) long, heads at 64°55'35" N, 145°33'14" W, flows NNW to the Middle Fork Chena River 19.3 km. (12 mi.) ESE of Chena Hot Springs; named for August Lohi (1895-1977), trapper and gold miner who, for 35 years, lived along the Middle Fork Chena River and built and maintained many miles of trails and numerous bridges throughout the area; sec. 22, T 2 N, R 10 E, Fairbanks Mer.; 64°58'50" N, 145°41'00" W. BGN 8301.

LONDON, MOUNT — peak, elevation 7,550 ft., in the Coast Mountains, on the Alaska-Canada boundary 7.5 mi. SE of Mount Poletica; named for the author, Jack London; sec. 3, T 33 S, R 66 E, Copper River Mer.; 59°02'22" N, 134°22'47" W. Not: Boundary Peak 100. BGN 1972.

LONESOME HILLS — hills, 12.9 km. (8 mi.) long and 9.7 km. (6 mi.) wide, highest elevation 526 m. (1,726 ft.), 22.5 km. (14 mi.) W of Medfra; bound on the E by Wabash Creek and on the SW by Broken Snowshoe Creek; so named because the hills are surrounded by the Nixon Fork lowlands; Tps. 27 and 28 S, Rgs. 19 and 20 E, Kateel River Mer.; 63°07'45" N, 155°14'55" W (center). BGN 8402.

Long Bay — estuary, see Nahku Bay.

LONG LAKE — lake, 0.4 mi. long, in the Aleutian Islands, on Amchitka Island 1.7 mi. NNE of Grampus Point and 1.9 mi. S of Jones Lake; 51°22'11" N, 170°16'05" E. BGN 1969.

Longmare Lake — lake, see Longmere Lake.

LONGMERE LAKE — lake, 3.7 km. (2.3 mi.) long, on the Kenai Peninsula, 6.4 km. (4 mi.) E of Soldotna; named by homesteader Don Culver in 1947; Kenai Peninsula Borough; secs. 19, 20, 29, 30 and 31,T 5 N, R 9 W, Seward Mer.; 60°30'00" N, 150°54'35" W; 1953 decision revised. Not: De Long Lake, Longmare Lake (BGN 1953), Longmore Lake. BGN 8504.

Longmore Lake — lake, see Longmere Lake.

Lonieof Lake — lake, see Maksoutof Lake.

LOON LAKE — lake, 0.8 km. (0.5 mi.) long on the Kenai Peninsula, drains NW to Bear Cove and Kachemak Bay; secs. 28 and 29, T 5 S, R 10 W, Seward Mer.; 59°42'50" N, 151°00'30" W. BGN 8001.

LOON SHOAL — shoal, 7.2 km. (4.5 mi.) long, in the Beaufort Sea 8 km. (5 mi.) NE of the Jones Islands; named for the U.S. Geological Survey research vessel Loon, which was used in scientific studies of the shoal; North Slope Borough; 70°35'18" N, 149°12'12" W (NW end), 70°34'00" N, 148°59'18" W (SE end). BGN 7902.

LOONSONG LAKE — lake, 1 km. (0.6 mi.) across, E of Anna Lake and W of Sevenmile Lake, 11.6 km. (7.2 mi.) W of Knik; Matanuska-Susitna Bor.; secs. 14 and 23, T 16 N, R 4 W, Seward Mer.; 61°28'04" N, 149°56'51" W. BGN 8301.

LOST LAKE — lake, 183 m. (600 ft.) long, 1.6 km. (1 mi.) W of the Taiya River and 7.5 km. (4.7 mi.) NNW of Skagway; so named because the lake is in a secluded area; sec. 21, T 27 S, R 59 E, Copper River Mer.; 59°31'00" N, 135°22'42" W. BGN 8501.

Lowell Island — island, see Fox Island.

LOWELL WAKEFIELD, MOUNT — peak, elevation 731 m. (2,400 ft.), on Raspberry Island 1.9 km. (1.2 mi.) W of Port Wakefield; named for Lowell A Wakefield (?-1977), who is credited with starting the Alaskan King Crab fishing industry in the United States, and who founded the Wakefield Fisheries; sec. 32, T 24 S, R 23 W, Seward Mer.; 58°03'00" N, 153°05'10" W. BGN 7804.

Lower Russian Mission — settlement, see Chuathbaluk.

LOWER SWEETHEART LAKE — lake, 5 mi. long, 12 mi. NW of Mount Sumdum and 35 mi. SE of Juneau; 57°58'15" N, 133°35'00" W. Not: Gilbert Lake, Sweetheart Lake (former decision). 1955. BGN 1967.

LUELIA, LAKE — lake, 1.7 mi. long, on Prince of Wales Island 4 mi. SE of Eudora Mountain; 55°04'00" N, 132°11'15" W. BGN 1969.

LULU FAIRBANKS, MOUNT — mountain, elevation 557 m. (1,827 ft.), 14.5 km. (9 mi.) NE of Fairbanks; named for Lulu Fairbanks (1888-1968), associate editor of the *Alaska Weekly* in Seattle and a member of the International Sourdoughs for 37 years; sec. 3, T 1 N, R 1 E, Fairbanks Mer.; 64°56'48" N, 147°32'00" W. BGN 7804.

LUTRIS PASS — water passage, 0.32 km. (0.2 mi.) wide, extends W from Heather Bay to Columbia Bay between S end of Heather Island to an unnamed island 1.3 km. (0.3 mi.) WNW of Elf Point and 21 km. (13 mi.) NW of Ellamar; secs. 31 and 32, T 10 S, R 10 W, Copper River Mer.; 60°57'50" N, 147°03'30" W. BGN 8003.

McCarty Arm	fiord, see McCarty Fiord.
MCCARTY FIORD	fiord, 34 km. (21 mi.) long, on the S coast of Kenai Peninsula, heads at McCarty Glacier at 59°43'45" N, 150°13'30" W, trends SSW to Nuka Bay at Harrington Point 72 km. (45 mi.) E of Seldovia; 59°27'45" N, 150°26'00" W; 1929 decision revised. Not: East Arm Nuka Bay (BGN 1929), McCarty Arm. BGN 8003.
McHENRY ISLET	island, 81 m. (264 ft.) long, off the W coast of Etolin Island, in McHenry Inlet 2.7 km. (1.7 mi.) ENE of Range Island; 56°00'37" N, 132°24'54" W. BGN 7704.
McHUGH PEAK	peak, elevation 4,301 ft., in the Chugach Mountains, 3.4 mi. S of Flattop Mountain and 14 mi. SE of Anchorage; 61°02'30" N, 149°39'50" W. 1942. BGN 1969.
MCKEON ROCK	rock, at the entrance of Neptune Bay, 2.2 km. (1.4 mi.) NE of McKeon Flats and 5.6 km. (3.5 mi.) SE of Homer Spit, Kenai Peninsula Bor.; sec. 19, T 7 S, R 12 W, Seward Mer., 59°33'09" N, 151°23'32" W. BGN 8401.
MCLEOD LAKE	lake, 0.8 km. (0.5 mi.) long, 2.6 km. (1.6 mi.) SW of Lost Cabin Lake and 11.5 km. (7.1 mi.) E of Tazlina; named for Bruce Burns McLeod (1914-1975), who used the area for trapping, fishing, hunting, and recreation since 1950; secs. 6 and 7, T 3 N, R 5 W, and secs. 1 and 12, T 3 N, R 6 W, Copper River Mer.; 62°03'48" N, 146°12'00" W. BGN 8203.
McLEOD, POINT	point of land, in Muir Inlet at N end of Hunter Cove; named for Captain McLeod of the SS _Princess Maquinna_ which brought members of the Twelfth International Geological Congress to Glacier Inlet in 1913; 58°54'50" N, 136°06'30" W. Not: Peter Point. 1941. BGN 1972.
Magoffin Lake	lake, see Volkmar Lake.

MAGPIE PEAK   peak, elevation 5,812 ft., in Chugach
                                    Mountains 27 mi. SE of Anchorage;
                                    61°02'20" N, 149°09'59" W. BGN 1968.

Maiden Creek   stream, see Nade Creek.

MAKSOUTOF LAKE   lake, 2 mi. long and 0.5 mi. wide, on
                                    Baranof Island 20 mi. NW of Port
                                    Alexander; 56°30' N, 134°55' W. Not:
                                    Gar Lake, Lonieof Lake. BGN 1968.

MAKSOUTOF RIVER   stream, 12 mi. long, on Baranof Island,
                                    heads at 56°36' N, 134°47' W, flows SW
                                    to Sandy Bay 22 mi. NW of Port
                                    Alexander, 56°30'15" N, 134°58'15" W.
                                    BGN 1968.

MALASPINA LAKE   lake, 5 km. (3 mi.) wide and 14.5 km.
                                    (9 mi.) long, at SE edge of Malaspina
                                    Glacier 35 km. (22 mi.) NW of Yakutat;
                                    59°48'00" N, 140°10'00" W. BGN 7303.

MALLOTT, MOUNT   peak, elevation 1,055 m. (3,460 ft.),
                                    24.1 km. (15 mi.) NE of Yakutat; sec. 1,
                                    T 26 S, R 35 E, Copper River Mer.;
                                    59°41'47" N, 139°24'45" W. BGN 7702.

MANTY MOUNTAIN   mountain, elevation 962 m. (3,156 ft.),
                                    on Prince of Wales Island, 16.1 km. (10
                                    mi.) SE of Sweetwater Lake and 48 km.
                                    (30 mi.) NE of Craig; named for Mildred
                                    V. Manty (1911-1978), Public Health
                                    Nurse who served the Alaska Department
                                    of Health and Social Services in the
                                    Ketchikan area since 1963; secs. 26 and
                                    35, T 69 S, R 82 E, Copper River Mer.;
                                    55°51'05" N, 132°47'30" W. BGN 8102.

MAPTIGAK MOUNTAIN   mountain, elevation 6,400 ft., in the
                                    Endicott Mountains 5 mi. NE of Rumbling
                                    Mountain; named for Morry Maptigak (died
                                    1947), leader of a Numuit tribe in the
                                    area; 68°03'55" N, 151°00'30" W. BGN
                                    1969.

Martin Island   island, see Doctor Island.

MARY CREEK   stream, 1.6 km. (1 mi.) long, heads at 60°24'30" N, 144°08'55" W, flows E to Kushtaka Glacier 1.1 km. (0.7 mi.) N of Kushtaka Lake; sec. 14, T 17 S, R 7 E, Copper River Mer.; 60°24'18" N, 144°07'30" W. BGN 7504.

MATANUSKA PEAK   peak, elevation 1,857 m. (6,093 ft.), in the Chugach Mountains, 4.8 km. (3 mi.) SE of Lazy Mountain and 12.1 km. (7.5 mi.) E of Palmer; Matanuska-Susitna Borough; sec. 34, T 18 N, R 3 E, Seward Mer.; 61°36'15" N, 148°53'00" W (1969 description revised). BGN 8004.

Max's Mountain   peak, see Bauman Bump.

Mead River   village, see Atqasuk.

Meade River   village, see Atqasuk.

Meade River Village   village, see Atqasuk.

MERIDIAN LAKE   lake, 0.3 mi. long, 5 mi. S of Lakeview and 12 mi. N of Seward; 60°17'10" N, 149°21'50" W. BGN 1968.

MERMAID ISLAND   island, in Neptune Bay 13.7 km. (8.5 mi.) SE of Homer; sec. 30, T 7 S, R 12 W, Seward Mer.; 59°32'34" N, 151°23'50" W. BGN 7504.

MERRI BELLE LAKE   lake, 244 m. (800 ft.) across, on E edge of the Meadow Lakes 7.2 km. (4.5 mi.) NW of Wasilla; Matanuska-Susitna Bor.; sec. 25, T 18 N, R 2 W, Seward Mer.; 61°37'05" N, 149°33'20" W. BGN 8301.

MEX ISLAND   island, 0.1 mi. across, 0.1 mi. off the S coast of Amchitka Island 8 mi. NW of Rifle Range Point; named for the triangulation station on the island; 51°28'26" N, 179°01'55" E. BGN 1972.

MIAMI LAKE   lake, 1.6 km. (1 mi.) long, 5.6 km. (3.5 mi.) S of Chulitna Pass; secs. 14 and 23, T 32 N, R 2 W, Seward Mer.; 62°51'00" N, 149°35'25" W. BGN 7402.

MIDDEN COVE	cove, 0.7 mi. long, in the Aleutian Islands, on the N coast of Amchitka Island 1.5 mi. E of Burr House Cove; named for the Aleut midden complex located at the southwest corner of the cove; 51°37'53" N, 178°46'50" E. BGN 1969.
MIDDEN POINT	point of land, in the Aleutian Islands, on the N coast of Amchitka Island 1 mi. NE of Burr House Cove; name is taken from the cove of the same name; 51°38'48" N, 178°45'47" E. BGN 1969.
MIDDLE BAY	bay, 3.2 km. (2 mi.) wide, on the SW coast of Kodiak Island, 3.8 km. (2.4 mi.) SSE of Middle Cape and 32 km. (20 mi.) SW of Karluk; Kodiak Island Borough; T 33 S, Rgs. 34 and 35 W, Seward Mer.; 57°19'15" N, 154°45'15" W. BGN 8203.
MIDDLE FORK CHENA RIVER	stream, 85 km. (53 mi.) long, heads at 65°05'32" N, 144°43'25" W, flows WSW to the Chena River 69 km. (43 mi.) ENE of Fairbanks; sec. 2, T 1 N, R 7 E, Fairbanks Mer.; 64°56'28" N, 146°15'05" W; 1965 decision revised. Variants: Chena River; East Fork Chena River (former decision). BGN 7402.
MIDNIGHT CREEK	stream, 5 mi. long, on the Seward Peninsula, heads at 65°48'25" N, 164°32'04" W, flows SE to Taylor Creek 12 mi. ENE of Taylor; 65°44'48" N, 164°27'37" W. Not: Kennedy Creek. 1901. BGN 1966.
MINK ISLAND	island, 1.6 km. (1 mi.) long, in Port Nellie Juan 5.6 km. (3.5 mi.) SW of Applegate Island; secs. 20, 21, 28, and 29, T 6 N, R 7 E, Seward Mer.; 60°35'25" N, 148°14'35" W. BGN 8002.
MINTO	populated place, along the Tolovana River 56 km. (35 mi.) SW of Livengood; secs. 22, 23, and 26, T 4 N, R 9 W, Fairbanks Mer.; 65°09'10" N, 149°20'20" W. Not: Minto Landing, Minto Roadhouse, Minto Telegraph Station. BGN 7702.

Minto Landing   populated place, see Minto.

Minto Roadhouse   populated place, see Minto.

Minto Telegraph Station   populated place, see Minto.

MOLVER ISLAND   island, 0.48 km. (0.3 mi.) long, off the NW end of Etolin Island, in Stikine Strait 32 km. (20 mi.) SW of Wrangell; named for John Ragnvard Molver (1880-1956), prominent member of the community of Petersburg, and leader in the local fishing industry; sec. 14, T 65 S, R 82 E, Copper River Mer.; 56°14'18" N, 132°41'39" W. BGN 8203.

MONARCH, MOUNT   peak, elevation 7,108 ft., in the Talkeetna Mountains 19 mi. ENE of Chickaloon; 61°54'18" N, 147°55'45" W. BGN 1972.

MONTAGUE STRAIT   water passage, 74 km. (46 mi.) long, and 19.3 km. (12 mi.) wide, extends SW from Prince William Sound to the Gulf of Alaska between Montague Island to the E and Knight and Latouche Islands to the W; 59°52'00" N, 147°58'00" W (SW end), 60°27'00" N, 147°22'00" W (NE end). Variant: Prince William Sound. BGN 7803.

MONTANA LAKE   lake, 0.7 mi. long, 13 mi. S of Talkeetna; 62°08'38" N, 150°02'58" W. Not: Little Bill Lake. BGN 1969.

Moores Creek   stream, see Captain William Moore Creek.

MOOSE CREEK   stream, 5.1 km. (3.2 mi.) long, heads at 57°46'52" N, 155°24'30" W, flows E to Little Alinchak Bay 16.9 km. (10.5 mi.) SW of Mount Kubugakli and 56 km. (35 mi.) WNW of Karluk; sec. 10, T 28, S, R 37 W, Seward Mer., 57°46'35" N, 155°19'45" W. BGN 8401.

MOOSE HILL   mountain, elevation 308 m. (1,012 ft.), between Jones Creek and its North Fork 3.5 km. (2.2 mi.) SSE of Denagiemina Lake and 23 km. (14 mi.) E of Nikolai; sec. 33, T 28 S, R 26 E, Kateel River Mer.; 63°01'28" N, 153°55'15" W. BGN 8401.

Mount Adolph Knopf	peak, see Ernest Gruening, Mount.
Mount Brack	mountain, see Brock, Mount.
Mount Genet	peak, see Church, Mount.
Mount Rasmussen	mountain, see Rasmusson Mount.
Mount Sentry	mountain, see Sovereign Mountain.
Mount Trident	mountain, see Trident Volcano.
Mount Waw	mountain, see Deliverance, Mount.
Mount Willard Gibbs	mountain, see Thor, Mount.
MUD BAY	cove, 0.64 km. (0.4 mi.) across, on W side of Keku Strait 32 km. (20 mi.) SE of Kake; sec. 4, T 60 S, R 74 E, Copper River Mer.; 56°41'38" N, 133°45'40" W. BGN 7704.
MUD CREEK	stream, 6.4 km. (4 mi.) long, on Kuiu Island, heads at 56°43'20" N, 133°50'00" W, flows SE to Mud Bay 32 km. (20 mi.) SE of Kake; sec. 4, T 60 S, R 74 E, Copper River Mer.; 56°41'40" N, 133°45'50" W. BGN 7704.
Mud Lake	lake, see Tern Lake.
Mumtrahamut	populated place, see Goodnews Bay.
Mumtrahamute	populated place, see Goodnews Bay.
Mumtrak	populated place, see Goodnews Bay.
Mumtrakmut	populated place, see Goodnews Bay.
Munto	populated place, see Old Minto.
MURDO ISLAND	island, 0.16 km. (0.1 mi.) long, in Port Chester 2.2 km. (1.4 km.) NNW of Metlakatla; T 78 S, R 92 E, Copper River Mer.; 55°08'57" N, 131°34'59" W. Not: Battleship Island, Murdo Islet. BGN 7903.
Murdo Islet	island, see Murdo Island.

MYRTLE CREEK	stream, 1.7 mi. long, on Prince of Wales Island, heads at 55°05'07" N, 132°09'23" W, flows SE through Myrtle Lake, to Niblack Anchorage 26 mi. SW of Ketchikan; 55°04'08" N, 132°07'53" W. BGN 1969.
Mys Kitovyy	point of land, see Kitovi Point.
Mys Polovinnoy	point of land, see Polovina Point.
Mys Tonkiy	point of land, see Stony Point.
Mys Yelovoy	point of land, see Ouzinkie Point.
MYSTERY HILLS	hills, highest elevation 3,520 ft., trend NW-SE for 5 mi. between the headwaters of Mystery Creek, on the NE, and Jean Creek, on the SW, 30 mi. E of Soldotna; 60°33'15" N, 150°11'15" W (NW end), 60°30'00" N, 150°03'30" W (SE end). BGN 1969.

NADEN CREEK   stream, 2.7 km. (1.7 mi.) long, heads at 63°04'00" N, 156°31'45" W, flows N to Spruce Creek 5.9 km. (3.7 mi.) S of Ophir; sec. 2, T 28 S, R 12 E, Kateel River Mer.; 63°05'28" N, 156°31'33" W. Not: Maiden Creek. BGN 8402.

NAHKU BAY   estuary, 1.9 km. (1.2 mi.) long and 0.48 km. (0.3 mi.) wide, at the head of Taiya Inlet 1.6 km. (1 mi.) NW of Skagway; 59°27'45" N, 135°20'20" W. Not: Long Bay. BGN 8501.

NANCY LAKE   lake, 5.6 km. (3.5 mi.) long, 4.8 km. (3 mi.) SE of Willow and 51 km. (32 mi.) N of Anchorage; Matanuska-Susitna Borough; Tps. 18 and 19 N, R 4 W, Seward Mer.; 61°41'15" N, 150°00'00" W; 1978 decision revised. Not: Lake Nancy (BGN 1978). BGN 8002.

Napaiskak   village, see Napaskiak.

Napaiskak Slough   stream, see Napaskiak Slough.

Napasiak   village, see Napaskiak.

Napaskiagamut   village, see Napaskiak.

Napaskiagamute   village, see Napaskiak.

NAPASKIAK   village, on left bank of the Kuskokwim River 6 mi. S of Bethel; 60°42'30" N, 161°45'50" W; 1941 decision revised. Not: Napaiskak (former decision), Napasiak, Napaskiagamut, Napaskiagamute, Napiakmut. BGN 1971.

NAPASKIAK SLOUGH   stream, 2.5 mi. long, heads at the junction of Tupuknuk Slough and an unnamed stream at 60°42'40" N, 161°45'55" W. Not: Napaiskak Slough. BGN 1971.

Napiakmut   village, see Napaskiak.

Narrow Point   point of land, see Stony Point.

NEACOLA MOUNTAINS	mountains, 130 km. (81 mi.) long, in the Aleutian Range, extend SW between Telaquana River, Neacola River, Chakachamna Lake, and Chakachatna River on the NW and Blockage Lake and Tlikakila River on the SE; named for the Neacola River which drains the highest and most rugged peaks of the mountains; 61°10'00" N, 152°00'00" W (NE end), 60°37'00" N, 154°05'00" W (SW end). Variant: Chigmit Mountains. BGN 7603.
NEAR POINT	peak, elevation 930 m. (3,052 ft.), in the Chugach Mountains, 3.2 km. (2 mi.) NW of Wolverine Peak and 8 km. (5 mi.) SE of Anchorage; so named because it is near Anchorage; Municipality of Anchorage; sec. 4, T 12 N, R 2 W, Seward Mer.; 61°09'19" N, 149°39'00" W. BGN 8103.
NEEG ISLAND	island, 0.32 km. (0.2 mi.) long, in Yakutat Bay 23.3 km. (14.5 mi.) NE of Yakutat; Neeg is reportedly a Tlingit Indian name meaning "small fort"; sec. 29, T 25 S, R 35 E, Copper River Mer.; 59°43'32" N, 139°31'08" W. BGN 7702.
NEGROMOON	creek, tributary to the Inglutalik River from the west, NE of Norton Bay, VACATED. 1910. BGN 1966.
NEKLASON LAKE	lake, 1.6 km. (1 mi.) long, 9.7 km. (6 mi.) NE of Wasilla; 61°37'45" N, 149°16'15" W. Not: Nicklason Lake, Niklason Lake. BGN 7902.
NELSON LAGOON	populated place, on a spit between Nelson Lagoon and Bristol Bay 38 km. (24 mi.) W of Port Moller; sec. 25, T 48 S, R 77 W, Seward Mer.; 56°00'03" N, 161°12'00" W. Not: Nelson Lagoon Village. BGN 8002.
Nelson Lagoon Village	populated place, see Nelson Lagoon.
New Andreafski	populated place, see Saint Marys.
New Andreafsky	populated place, see Saint Marys.

New Knock Hock	village, see New Knockhock.
NEW KNOCKHOCK	village, on the right bank of the Black River, 12 mi. NW of the Kusilvak Mountains and 38 mi. W of Mountain Village; 62°07'30" N, 164°53'30" W. Not: New Knock Hock. 1950. BGN 1966.
NIBLACK LAKE	lake, 1.8 mi. long, on Prince of Wales Island 25 mi. SW of Ketchikan; 55°05'30" N, 132°08'30" W. BGN 1969.
Nicklason Lake	lake, see Neklason Lake.
NIGU HILLS	hills, highest elevation 3,000 ft., 5 mi. long and 4 mi. wide, in the Brooks Range, on the N side of the Howard Hills 12 mi. NE of Howard Pass; 68°23' N, 156°33' W. 1966. BGN 1967.
Nikishka	locality, see Nikishka Number Two.
Nikishka	populated place, see Nikiski.
Nikishka	populated place, see Port Nikiski.
Nikishka 1	populated place, see Port Nikiski.
Nikishka Bay	bight, see Nikiski Bay.
Nikishka No. 1	locality, see Nikishka.
Nikishka Number One	populated place, see Port Nikiski.
NIKISHKA NUMBER TWO	locality, on NW coast of Kenai Peninsula 19.3 km. (12 mi.) N of Kenai; secs. 35 and 36, T 8 N, R 12 W, Seward Mer.; 60°44'20" N, 151°19'30" W. Variants: Nikishka, Nikishki, Nikiski Wharf. BGN 7501.
Nikishka Number Two	populated place, see Nikiski.
Nikishki	locality, see Nikishka Number Two.
Nikishki Bay	bight, see Nikiski Bay.
Nikiska Bay	bight, see Nikiski Bay.

NIKISKI	populated place, area of approximately 72 sq. km. (45 sq. mi.), on NW section of the Kenai Peninsula 15.3 km. (9.5 mi.) N of Kenai; Kenai Peninsula Borough; 60°41'25" N, 151°17'20" W. Not: Nikishka, Nikishka Number Two, North Kenai. BGN 8504.
Nikiski	populated place, see Port Nikiski.
NIKISKI BAY	bight, 6.4 km. (4 mi.) across, on NW coast of the Kenai Peninsula, extends SW from Boulder Point, 20.9 km. (13 mi.) N of Kenai; Kenai Peninsula Borough; 60°44'45" N, 151°18'00" W; 1951 decision revised. Not: Nikishka Bay (BGN 1951), Nikishki Bay (BGN 1916), Nikiska Bay. BGN 8504.
Nikiski Wharf	locality, see Nikishka Number Two.
Nikiski Wharf	populated place, see Port Nikiski.
Niklason Lake	lake, see Neklason Lake.
Ningaluk River	channel, see Ninglick River.
NINGLICK RIVER	channel, 35 km. (22 mi.) long, heads in Baird Inlet at 60°50'30" N, 164°32'15" W, flows W to Hazen Bay N of Kigigak Island; 60°53'45" N, 165°01'30" W. Variants: Nigaluk River, Ninglik Pass. BGN 7501.
Ninglik Pass	channel, see Ninglick River.
NIVAT POINT	point of land, in Kasegaluk Lagoon on NW coast of Alaska 3.2 km. (2 mi.) SW of Nokotlek Point; 70°18'30" N, 161°04'35" W. BGN 7802.
NO NAME ISLAND	island, 0.48 km. (0.3 mi.) long, in Blying Sound near the S end of the Aialik Penninsula on the Kenai Peninsula, 1.6 km. (1 mi.) NE of Aialik Cape; Kenai Peninsula Borough; 59°43'10" N, 149°30'30" W. BGN 8003.
No Name Island	island, see Bartlett Island.
Noluck Lake	lake, see Nullaq Lake.

Noluk Lake   lake, see Nullaq Lake.

Nooiksut   populated place, see Nuiqsut.

NORTH BIGHT   bay, 0.4 mi. across, in the Aleutian islands, on the N coast and at the SE end of Amchitka Island 0.8 mi. NE of South Bight and 2.3 mi. WNW of East Cape; 51°23'10" N, 170°24'50" E. BGN 1969.

North Buttress   mountain, see Hesperus, Mount.

NORTH CRATER   crater, 0.32 km. (0.2 mi.) across, on Mount Wrangell 2.4 km. (1.5 mi.) W of its summit and 1.6 km. (1 mi.) N of Wrangell Crater; secs. 26 and 35, T 3 N, R 7 E, Copper River Mer.; 62°00'15" N, 144°03'45" W. BGN 8002.

NORTH CREEK   stream, 13.1 km. (8.1 mi.) long, heads at 57°55'07" N, 155°22'09" W, flows SE to Bear Bay 6.9 km. (4.3 mi.) WSW of Mount Kubugakli and 56 km. (35 mi.) NW of Karluk; sec. 6, T 27 S, R 36 W, Seward Mer.; 57°52'28" N, 155°14'45" W. BGN 8401.

NORTH FORK QUARTZ CREEK   stream, 3.5 mi. long, on the Seward Peninsula, heads at 65°24'30" N, 164°46'40" W, flows SE to Quartz Creek, 0.3 mi. NW of Dahl and 26 mi. SSE of Taylor; 65°22'05" N, 164°43'00" W. Not: Right Fork Quartz Creek. BGN 1902. BGN 1966.

North Fork Tanunak River   stream, see North Fork Tununak River.

NORTH FORK TUNUNAK RIVER   stream, 9.7 km. (6 mi.) long, heads at 60°35'05" N, 165°08'10" W, flows W to Tununak River at Tununak; sec. 28, T 6 N, R 91 W, Seward Mer.' 60°34'57" N, 165°15'10" W. Variant: North Fork Tanunak River. BGN 7603.

North Kenai   populated place, see Nikiski.

NORTH POINT SHOAL   shoal, 2.4 km. (1.5 mi.) long, in Knik Arm, 3.7 km. (2.3 mi.) NNE of North Point on Fire Island and 12.9 km. (8 mi.) W of Anchorage; Matanuska-Susitna Bor.; 61°13'06" N, 150°06'59" W (NE end), 61°12'30" N, 150°09'01" W (SW end). BGN 8501.

NORTHBIRD   peak, elevation, 1,022 mi. (3,350 ft.), on Revillagigedo Island between Granite Basin and Upper Silvis Lake 6 km. (3.7 mi.) NE of Ketchikan; named to commemorate earliest known active commercial aircraft which bore this name; 55°22'25" N, 131°33'56" W. BGN 7404.

NORTHWESTERN FIORD   fiord, 14.5 km. (9 mi.) long, on the S coast of Kenai Peninsula, heads at Northwestern Glacier and trends SE to Harris Bay 7.2 km. (4.5 mi.) NNW of Granite Island; 59°50'10" N, 150°03'10" W (NW end), 59°44'00" N, 149°54'00" W (SE end); 1978 decision revised. Not: Harris Bay, Northwestern Glacier, Northwestern Lagoon (BGN 1978). BGN 8003.

NORTHWESTERN GLACIER   glacier, 3.7 km. (2.3 mi.) long, heads in the Kenai Mountains at 59°51'50" N, 150°04'30" W, trends S to the head of Northwestern Fiord 8 km. (5 mi.) E of McCarty Glacier; named about 1909 by U.S. Grant (U.S. Geological Survey) for Northwestern University, Evanston, Illinois; 59°49'50" N, 149°04'00" W; 1910 description revised. BGN 8003.

Northwestern Glacier   fiord, see Northwestern Fiord.

NORTHWESTERN LAGOON   lagoon, 1.8 km. (1.1 mi.) long, on the S coast of Kenai Peninsula, at the SE end of Northwestern Fiord 8 km. (5 mi.) NW of Granite Island; secs. 21, 22, 27, and 28, T 5 S, R 4 W, Seward Mer.; 59°43'30" N, 149°57'40" W; 1978 description revised. BGN 8003.

Northwestern Lagoon   fiord, see Northwestern Fiord.

NUIQSUT   populated place (incorporated city), on the left bank of the Nechelik Channel of the Colville River 47 km. (29 mi.) SE of Atigaru Point and 105 km. (65 mi.) NE of Umiat; North Slope Bor.; sec. 8, T 10 N, R 5 E, Umiat Mer.; 70°13'03" N, 150°58'35" W. Not: Nooiksut. BGN 8402.

Nukiukahyet	village, see Nukluklayet.
NUKLUKLAYET	village, on the middle Yukon, about 20 mi. W of the mouth of Tanana River. Not: Nukiukahyet, Nuklukyet, Tuklukyet. VACATED. 1917. BGN 1966.
Nuklukyet	village, see Nukluklayet.
NULLAQ LAKE	lake, 4 km. (2.5 mi.) long, on the N slope of the De Long Mountains 29 km. (18 mi.) NNE of Black Mountain; Nullag is an Inupiaq Eskimo word meaning "this is the place we stay or camp tonight"; North Slope Bor.; Tps. 7 and 8 S, R 34 W, Umiat Mer.; 68°47'30" N, 160°00'00" W; 1961 decision revised. Not: Lake Noluck, Lake Noluk, Noluck Lake (BGN 1961, 1925), Noluk Lake. BGN 8402.
NUNAMUIT MOUNTAIN	mountain, elevation 6,509 ft., in the Brooks Range 8.5 mi. NW of the village of Anaktuvuk Pass; named for the Nunamuit Eskimo tribe who have inhabited the Brooks Range for 400 years; 68°11'00" N, 152°02'30" W. BGN 1969.
NUNAVACHAK BAY	bay, 6.7 km. (4.2 mi.) across, on the N shore of Bristol Bay 7.2 km. (4.5 mi.) NE of Summit Island; 58°52'00" N, 160°02'40" W. BGN 8504.
NUT ROCK	rock, off the W coast of Etolin Island, in McHenry Inlet 2.6 km. (1.6 mi.) E of Range Island; 56°00'20" N, 132°25'20" W. BGN 7704.

OLD VALDEZ   populated place, section of Valdez, on
                        E end of Port Valdez 5 km (3.1 mi.) SE
                        of center of City of Valdez; sec. 2 and
                        3, T 9 S, R 6 W, Copper River Mer.;
                        61°07'00" N, 146°16'00" W; 1904 decision
                        revised. Not: Valdes, Valdez (BGN
                        1904). BGN 8003.

Old Valdez   populated place, see Valdez.

OTTER LAKE   lake, 0.8 km. (0.5 mi.) long, 1.1 km.
                        (0.7 mi.) E of Alexander Creek 7.2 km.
                        (4.5 mi.) NW of Susitna; secs. 6 and 7,
                        T 17 N, R 7 W, Seward Mer.; 61°35'10" N,
                        150°37'10" W. BGN 8001.

PAINTER CREEK	stream, 20 mi. long, heads at 57°01'00" N, 157°25'30" W, flows N to King Salmon River 0.3 mi. W of Mother Goose Lake, on the Alaska Peninsula; 57°13'00" N, 157°24'15" W. Not: Jimmy Orr Creek. 1923. BGN 1967.
Palmer Creek	stream, see Bodenburg Creek.
PALUGVIK CREEK	stream, 5.6 km. (3.5 mi.) long, heads at 60°28'50" N, 146°08'50" W, flows SW to Hawkins Island Cutoff 21 km. (14 mi.) WSW of Cordova; sec. 25, T 16 S, R 6 W, Copper River Mer.; 60°27'28" N, 146°11'45" W. BGN 7403.
PARADISE PEAK	peak, elevation 6,050 ft. 4 mi. S of Mother Goose Glacier and 14 mi. NNE of Seward; named for Paradise Valley which it borders on the S; sec. 13, T 2 N, R 1 E, Seward Mer.; 60°16'04" N, 149°11'30" W. BGN 1971.
PARKA PEAK	peak, elevation 13,280 ft., in Wrangell Mountains 2 mi. E of Atna Peaks; 61°44'52" N, 143°10'15" W. Not: Ultima Peak. BGN 1968.
Parsons Peak	mountain, see Face Mountain.
PATRICK LAKE	lake, 1.3 km. (0.8 mi.) long, 32 km. (20 mi.) SW of Collinsville; secs. 4 and 5, T 24 N, R 14 W, Seward Mer.; 62°07'15" N, 151°52'00" W. BGN 7403.
PATTON RIVER	stream, 6 mi. long, on Montague Island, heads at 59°58'40" N, 147°33'10" W, flows SSE to Patton Bay 5.5 mi. N of Jeanie Point; 59°54'50" N, 147°29'55" W. BGN 1967.
PAUL, LAKE	lake, 300 ft. across, 3 mi. NNW of Fairbanks; named for Paul Palfy (died in 1965), former owner of the property, who came to Alaska in 1913; 64°53'12" N, 147°45'45" W. Not: Rat Lake. BGN 1969.

PAYNE ISLAND — island, 2.6 km. (1.6 mi.) long, largest of the Keku Islands, 11.6 km. (7.2 mi.) SW of Kake; named for Judge Payne, who had operated a fox farm on the island; secs. 6, 7, and 8, T 57 S, R 72 E, Copper River Mer.; 56°56'45" N, 134°07'30" W. BGN 7702.

Peekaboo Peak — mountain, see Peeking Mountain.

PEEKING MOUNTAIN — mountain, elevation over 6,900 ft., in Chugach Mountains 23 mi. ENE of Anchorage; 61°16'15" N, 149°11'30" W. Not: Peekaboo Peak. BGN 1968.

PENN CREEK — stream, 1.5 km. (0.9 mi.) long, heads at 60°24'53" N, 144°08'50" W, flows E to Kushtaka Glacier 1.6 km. (1 mi.) N of Kushtaka Lake; sec. 11, T 17 S, R 7 E, Copper River Mer.; 60°24'48" N, 144°07'20" W. BGN 7504.

PEREGRINE PASS — gap, elevation 1,585 m. (5,200 ft.), in the Endicott Mountains, 3.2 km. (2 mi.) NE of Als Mountain and 43 km. (27 mi.) ESE of the community of Anaktuvuk Pass; named for the peregrine falcons which reportedly nest in the cliffs near the top of the pass; North Slope Bor.; secs. 10 and 11, T 16 S, R 6 E, Umiat Mer.; 68°04'23" N, 150°41'45" W. BGN 8403.

PEREGRINE POINT — point of land, on N coast of Amchitka Island 0.81 km. (0.5 mi.) S of Chitka Point; there is a peregrine falcon eyrie located here; 51°34'30" N, 178°59'25" E. BGN 7504.

PERUE PEAK — peak, elevation 933 m. (3,060 ft.), on the NW end of Prince of Wales Island 6.1 km. (3.8 mi.) ENE of Mount Calder and 7.7 km. (4.8 mi.) NW of Red Bay Mountain; name recommended by local citizens in 1979 to honor Norman Perue (1940-1978), logger who lived and worked in the area for several years and died in an airplane crash 10 miles N of this feature; secs. 9, 10, 15, and 16, T 65 S, R 77 E, Copper River Mer.; 56°14'26" N, 133°29'45" W. BGN 8102.

Peter Point — point of land, see McLeod Point.

PETREL POINT — point of land, on N coast of Amchitka Island 11.3 km. (7 mi.) SE of Chitka Point; the petrel is a common bird in the area; 51°29'35" N, 179°05'40" E. BGN 7504.

PHELAN CREEK — stream, 20 mi. long, heads at Gulkana Glacier at 63°14'28" N, 145°28'00" W, flows NW to the Delta River 22 mi. NNW of Paxson; 63°20'00" N, 145°44'35" W. Not: Gulkana Creek, Gulkana River (former decision in part). 1898. BGN 1969.

PILLOW POINT — point of land, on the SE coast of Amchitka Island in the Aleutian Islands, 3 mi. W of Omega Point; named for nearby outcrops of pillow lavas; 51°21'45" N, 179°19'30" E. BGN 1969.

PINNYANAKTUK CREEK — stream, 6.7 km. (4.2 mi.) long, heads at 67°52'26" N, 150°35'15" W, flows SE to Clear River 40 km. (25 mi.) NNW of Nolan; from the Eskimo word meaning "absolute perfection of beauty"; 67°49'23" N, 150°31'50" W. Variant: Binnyanaktuk Creek. BGN 7402.

PIRATE LAKE — lake, 1.3 km. (0.8 mi.) long, in Denali National Park and Preserve, 3.2 km. (2 mi.) SE of Ruth Glacier and 38 km. (24 mi.) NNW of Talkeetna; named for Raymond Edward Genet(1931-1979), mountain climber and climbing guide who led numerous rescue missions on the slopes of Mount McKinley; his nickname was "Pirate"; Matanuska-Susitna Borough; secs. 26 and 35, T 30 N, R 6 W, Seward Mer.; 62°39'10" N, 150°20'05" W. BGN 8501.

Pistol Lake — lake, see Silver Salmon Lake.

PLUG MOUNTAIN — mountain, elevation 1,220 m. (4,000 ft.), 15 mi. SW of Mount Greenough; 69°04'40" N, 142°12'30" W. BGN 7501.

PLUNGE CREEK	stream, 14.5 km. (9 mi.) long, heads at 69°10'50" N, 146°15'40" W, flows NE to Canning River 16.1 km. (10 mi.) NE of Mount Salisbury; feature is in the area of a major plunging anticline; 69°15'40" N, 146°01'00" W. BGN 7501.
PLUTON COVE	cove, 0.6 mi. across, in the Aleutian Islands, at the SE end of Amchitka Island 1 mi. WSW of East Cape; named for the quartz diorite pluton found here; 51°22'05" N, 179°26'20" E. BGN 1969.
POINT CREEK	stream, 7.2 km. (4.5 mi.) long, heads at 63°39'03" N, 160°45'40" W, flows NW to Norton Sound 21.2 km. (13.2 mi.) SSW of Unalakleet; sec. 7, T 21 S, R 11 W, Kateel River Mer.; 63°41'27" N, 160°52'08" W. BGN 8103.
POINT RIOU SPIT	spit, 5.5 km. (3.4 mi.) long, extends NW and NE from Point Riou into Icy Bay forming Riou Bay 5 km. (3.1 mi.) SW of Moraine Island; secs. 14, 15 16, 21, 22, 27, and 34, T 25 S, R 23 E, Copper River Mer.; 59°54'30" N, 141°27'40" W. Not: Riou Spit. BGN 7902.
POLOVINA POINT	point of land, on E coast of Saint Paul Island in the Pribilof Islands 8 km. (5 mi.) NE of the village of Saint Paul; name derived from the Russian name Mys Polovinnoy meaning "Halfway Cape" and published by Tebenkov in 1852; 57°09'45" N, 170°10'15" W; 1978 decision revised. Not: Halfway Point (BGN 1978), Mys Polovinnoy. BGN 8103.
PORPHYRY HILL	hill, Fourth Judicial Division, about 1,200 ft. high; 62°13' N, 157°56' W. VACATED. 1945. BGN 1966.
PORT NIKISKI	populated place, section of Nikiski, on NW coast of Kenai Peninsula, on shore of Cook Inlet 16.1 km. (10 mi.) NNW of Kenai; Kenai Peninsula Borough; T 7 N, R 12 W, Seward Mer.; 60°41'00" N, 151°22'44" W; 1975 decision revised. Not: Bernice Lake, Nikishka (BGN 1975), Nikishka Number One, Nikishka 1, Nikiski, Nikiski Wharf. BGN 8504.

PORT WAKEFIELD	cove, 0.2 mi. wide, on NE coast of Kodiak Island, on W shore of Kizhuyak Bay 15 mi. NW of Kodiak; named for Lee Howard Wakefield (died 1954), owner and operator of numerous salmon canneries in Alaska; 57°51'45" N, 152°51'30" W. BGN 1968.
PRESTON CREEK	stream, 3.2 km. (2 mi.) long, on the Alaska Peninsula, heads at 57°16'50" N, 156°28'45" W, flows NE to Wide Bay 40.2 km. (25 mi.) SW of Kanatak; sec. 25, T 33 S, R 45 W, Seward Mer.; 57°18'10" N, 156°27'25" W. BGN 8104.
Prince William Sound	water passage, see Montague Strait.
Proliv Zimovya	water passage, see Zimovia Strait.
PTARMIGAN PEAK	peak, elevation 1,610 m. (5,280 ft.), 3.2 km. (2 mi.) NW of Suicide Peaks in the Chugach Mountains, and 17.7 km. (11 mi.) SE of Anchorage; Greater Anchorage Area Borough; sec. 10, T 11 N, R 2 W, Seward Mer.; 61°03'35" N, 149°36'10" W. BGN 8103.
PUGET PEAK	peak, elevation 3,931 ft., on Kenai Peninsula, 1.4 mi. NW of head of Puget Bay and 32 mi. E of Seward; 60°02'41" N, 148°34'57" W. BGN 1967.
PULLEN, MOUNT	peak, elevation 6,816 ft., in the Coast Mountains, on the Alaska-Canada boundary 4 mi. S of Mount Canning; named for Harriet Pullen, longtime resident of Skagway who arrived with the gold rush in 1897; sec. 8, T 31 S, R 64 E, Copper River Mer.; 59°11'32" N, 134°40'38" W. Not: Boundary Peak 104. BGN 1972.
PUYUK LAKE	lake, 0.48 km. (0.3 mi.) wide, one of the Clear Lakes on Saint Michaels Island 8.9 km. (5.5 mi.) NW of Saint Michael; Eskimo word meaning "smoke" in reference to the lake's volcanic origin; secs. 7 and 18, T 23 S, R 18 W, Kateel River Mer.; 63°30'12" N, 162°12'30" W. BGN 8002.
PYRAMID PEAK	peak, elevation 3,958 ft., 4 mi. NE of McKinley Peak and 22 mi. E of Cordova; 60°30"48" N, 145°07'00" W. BGN 1967.

QUIET LAKE   lake, 0.9 mi. long, 1.7 mi. SW of
                            Shulin Lake and 30 mi. SW of Talkeetna;
                            sec. 4, T 23 N, R 9 W, and sec. 33, T 24
                            N, R 9 W, Seward Mer.; 62°07'00" N,
                            150°55'15" W. BGN 1972.

QUONSET LAKE   lake, 0.25 mi. across, in the Aleutian
                            Islands, on Amchitka Island 2.3 mi. NNE
                            of Rifle Range Point and 2.5 mi. S of
                            Crown Reefer Point; named for World War
                            II quonset huts located at edge of lake;
                            51°25'57" N, 179°11'05" E. BGN 1969.

RAATIKAINEN, MOUNT	peak, elevation 1,101 m. (3,613 ft.), on Chichagof Island 4.8 km. (3 mi.) SW of Pelican, named for Kalle Raatikainen (1888-1959), fisherman and businessman who founded the village of Pelican - named for his boat - by locating a cold storage fish plant there in 1938; sec. 36, T 45 S, R 56 E, Copper River Mer.; 57°55'50" N, 136°16'25" W. BGN 7503.
RAINIER ISLAND	island, 0.16 km. (0.1 mi.) long, in Freshwater Bay 5.1 km. (3.2 mi.) NW of the Redcliff Islands and 16.1 km. (10 mi.) N of the village of Tenakee Springs; named by the National Ocean Survey for the National Oceanic and Atmospheric Administration survey vessel *Rainier*, used in Hydrographic studies of this area in May and June of 1979; 58°55'40" N, 135°11'00" W. BGN 8103.
RAM GLACIER	glacier, 10 mi. long, heads on W side of Mount Tittman at 61°07' N, 141°15' W, trends SW to a point 0.8 mi. N of Chitina Glacier and 60 mi. SE of McCarthy; 61°00'42" N, 141°25'00" W. BGN 1967.
Rasmussen Glacier	glacier, see Rasmusson Glacier.
RASMUSSON GLACIER	glacier, 4 km. (2.5 mi.) long, heads on N slope of Mount Rasmusson, trends N 1.1 km. (0.7 mi.) then SE to its 1959 terminus 1.6 km. (1 mi.) W of Russel Fiord and 34 km. (21 mi.) NE of Yakutat; named in 1905 by Ralph S. Tarr and Lawrence Martin for E. A. Rasmusson, teacher at the government school at Yakutat and missionary of the Swedish Evangelical Mission Convenant of American Society; sec. 6, T 25 S, R 36 E, Copper River Mer.; 59°47'00" N, 139°23'30" W; 1978 description revised. Not: Rasmussen Glacier. BGN 8102.

RASMUSSON, MOUNT	mountain, elevation 1,158 m. (3,800 ft.), on Puget Peninsula 4.3 km. (2.7 mi.) SE of Mount Hendrickson and 32 km. (20 mi.) NE of Yakutat; named in 1905 by Ralph S. Tarr and Lawrence Martin for E. A. Rasmusson, teacher at the government school at Yakutat and missionary of the Swedish Evalgelical Mission Convenant of America; sec. 33, T 24 S, R 35 E, Copper River Mer.; 59°47'10" N, 139°25'40" W; 1978 decision revised. Not: Mount Rasmussen, Rasmusson Mountain. BGN 8102.
Rasmusson Mountain	mountain, see Rasmusson, Mount.
Rat Lake	lake, see Paul, Lake.
READY BULLION CREEK	stream, 13.7 km. (8.5 mi.) long, heads 11.3 km. (7 mi.) NNW of Mount Joaquin at 62°57'30" N, 156°18'10" W, flows N to the Innoko River 12.9 km. (8 mi.) SE of Ophir; sec. 14, T 28 S, R 13 E, Kateel River Mer.; 63°03'53" N, 156°19'35" W; 1936 decision revised. Not: Independence Creek (BGN 1936). BGN 8402.
REDCLIFF ISLANDS	islands, includes West and East Redcliff Islands, in Freshwater Bay 14.5 km. (9 mi.) NE of the village of Tenakee Springs; 57°53'55" N, 135°06'30" W; 1978 description revised. BGN 8103.
REDWACKE CREEK	stream, 20.9 km. (13 mi.) long, heads at 69°28'25" N, 142°29'10" W, flows N to Egaksrak River 43 km. (27 mi.) W of Demarcation Point; sec. 6, T 3 N, R 40 E, Umiat Mer.; 69°38'50" N, 142°23'50" W. BGN 7501
Reference Lake	lake, see Sacred Lake.
Renard Island	island, see Fox Island.
RESURRECTION PEAKS	peaks, highest elevation 4,712 ft., trend N-S on the N side of Resurrection River 5 mi. N of Seward; 60°13'30" N, 149°28'20" W (N end), 60°10'45" N, 149°27'30" W (S end). Not: Sheep Mountain. BGN 1969.

REVELATION GLACIER   glacier, 10 mi. long, in Revelation Mountains, heads at 61°39'55" N, 154°10'45" W, trends N to an unnamed tributary of the Big River 17 mi. NW of Mount Mausolus; 61°48'15" N, 154°11'55" W. BGN 1968.

REVELATION MOUNTAINS   mountains, extend N-S 26 mi. in the Alaska Range 110 mi. NW of Tyonek; bounded on N and NE by the Big River and on SE and S by the Swift River; 61°53' N, 154°27' W (N end), 61°28' N, 154°15' W (S end). BGN 1968.

REYNARD, POINT   point of land, on Chichagof Island on W side of South Arm Hoonah Sound at N entrance to Patterson Bay 22.5 km. (14 mi.) E of Chichagof; named in 1895 by Lt. William I. Moore, U.S. Navy, for the Coast Survey steam launch *Reynard*; sec. 28, T 48 S, R 60 E, Copper River Mer.; 57°40'23" N, 135°42'40" W. BGN 7704.

RIFLE RANGE POINT   point of land, in the Aleutian Islands, on the S coast of Amchitka Island 2.8 mi. NW of Saint Makarius Point; named for the World War II rifle range located just inland from the point; 51°23'51" N, 179°10'14" E. BGN 1969.

Right Fork Quartz Creek   stream, see North Fork Quartz Creek.

RIGHT MOUNTAIN   mountain, elevation 1,550 m. (5,085 ft.), 2.4 km. (1.5 mi.) W of Crescent Lake and 40 km. (25 mi.) NNW of Seward; secs. 3 and 4, T 4 N, R 2 W, Seward Mer.; 60°28'15" N, 149°37'00" W. BGN 7802.

RIM POINT   point of land, in the Aleutian Islands, at the W end and on the S coast of Amchitka Island 4.6 mi. SE of Aleut Point; named for the triangulation station located here; 51°35'35" N, 178°42'10" E. BGN 1969.

Riou Spit   spit, see Point Riou Spit.

ROAD ISLAND   island, 1 mi. long, in Ivanof Bay on the S side of Alaska Peninisula, 13 mi. WSW of Perryville; 55°50'45" N, 159°29'45" W. Not: John Island. 1947. BGN 1967.

ROBERT KORN, MOUNT	peak, elevation 2,979 ft., in the Heney Range 4 mi. S of Cordova; named for Robert Wade Korn (1891-1972), pioneer Alaskan and former mayor of Cordova; sec. 16, T 16 S, R 3 W, Copper River Mer.; 60°29'17" N, 145°46'34" W. BGN 1972.
Rochers Kilikak	rocks, see Kilokak Rocks.
ROCKY MOUNTAIN	mountain, elevation 1,543 m. (5,062 ft.), 22.5 km. (14 mi.) NW of Mount Prindle and 113 km. (70 mi.) WSW of Circle, Yukon-Koyukuk Bor.; sec. 5, T 9 N, R 5 E, Fairbanks Mer., 65°38'00" N, 146°45'20" W. Not: Lime Peak. BGN 8401.
Rocky Point	point of land, see Stony Point.
ROY JONES MOUNTAIN	mountain, elevation 1,000 m. (3,280 ft.), on Revillagigedo Island 5.6 km. (3.5 mi.) NE of Ketchikan; named for Roy Franklin Jones (died 1974), who in 1922 piloted the first commercial flight to Alaska; sec. 15, T 75 S, R 91 SE, Copper River Mer.; 55°22'12" N, 131°34'07" W. BGN 7504.
RUDDY MOUNTAIN	mountain, elevation 2,289 m. (7,510 ft.), in the Wrangell Mountains 40 km. (25 mi.) E of Glennallen; secs. 31 and 36, T 4 N, R 3 E, and T 4 N, R 4 E, Copper River Mer.; 62°05'18" N, 144°45'55" W. BGN 7902.
Russian Mission	settlement, see Chuathbaluk.
Ruth Amphitheater	basin, see Don Sheldon Amphitheater.
Ruth Amphitheatre	basin, see Don Sheldon Amphitheater.
RYAN LAKE	lake, 0.3 km. (0.2 mi.) long, 1.6 km. (1 mi.) N of Grassy Lake and 3.7 km. (2.3 mi.) SE of Unalakleet; sec. 12, T 19 S, R 11 W, Kateel River Mer.; 63°51'10" N, 160°43'30: W. BGN 8103.
Ryan Lake	lake, see Grassy Lake.

SACRED LAKE   lake, 0.81 km. (0.5 mi.) long, S of Icy Bay and 3.2 km. (2 mi.) E of Point Riou; sec. 36, T 23 S, R 23 E, Copper River Mer.; 59°52'55" N, 141°24'10" W. Not: Reference Lake (BGN 1978). BGN 8001.

SAINT HERMAN BAY   bay, 1.3 km. (0.8 mi.) long, in Saint Paul Harbor 0.8 km. (0.5 mi.) SW of Kodiak; bound on the NW by Gull and Uski Islands and on the SE by Near Island; Kodiak Island Bor.; T 28 S, R 20 W, Seward Mer.; 57°46'40" N, 152°24'45" W. Not: Dog Bay. BGN 8402.

SAINT MAKARIUS POINT   peninsula, 0.2 mi. across, in the Aleutian Islands, on the S coast of Amchitka Island 1 mi. S of Makarius Bay and 1.4 mi. NW of Grampus Point; named by personnel of the USS *Oglala* in 1935, in the belief that Amchitka Island was the island Vitus Bering saw and named Saint Makarius in 1741; 51°21'45" N, 179°12'50" E. BGN 1937. BGN 1969.

Saint Makarius Point   point of land, see Grampus Point.

SAINT MARYS   populated place (incorporated city), on the W shore of Andreafsky River 6.4 km. (4 mi.) ENE of Pitkas Point and 29 km. (18 mi.) E of Mountain Village; sec. 26, T 23 N, R 76 W, Seward Mer.; 62°03'10" N, 162°10'00" W; 1931 decision revised. Not: Andreafski, Andreafsky (BGN 1931), Andreaoffsky, New Andreafski, New Andreafsky. BGN 8402.

SALISBURY CREEK   stream, 19.3 km. (12 mi.) long, heads at 69°05'30" N, 146°16'15" W, flows ENE to Marsh Fork Canning River 16.1 km. (10 mi.) E of Mount Salisbury; 69°09'00" N, 145°52'30" W. BGN 7504.

SALLY LAKE   lake, 1.1 km. (0.7 mi.) long, in the Talkeetna Mountains, 0.97 km. (0.6 mi.) N of the Susitna River and 77 km. (48 mi.) E of the community of Gold Creek; Matanuska-Susitna Borough; sec. 29, T 32 N, R 7 E, Seward Mer.; 62°50'05" N, 148°11'00" W. BGN 8502.

SALT CHUCK   bay, 1.9 km. (1.2 mi.) long, on Chichagof Island, on the S shore of Port Frederick 22.5 km. (14 mi.) SW of Hoonah, "chuck" is a Chinook jargon word meaning "water", Sitka Bor.; secs. 22, 23, and 27, T 45 S, R 60 E, Copper River Mer.; 57°57'00" N, 135°39'40" W. Not: Salt Lake Bay. BGN 8401.

SALT LAKE BAY   bay, 2.6 km. (1.6 mi.) long, on Chichagof Island, on the S shore of Port Frederick 20.4 km. (12.7 mi.) SW of Hoonah, Sitka Bor.; secs. 11, 14, 15, and 23, T 45 S, R 60 E, Copper River Mer.; 57°58'00" N, 135°39'00" W. BGN 8401.

Salt Lake Bay   bay, see Salt Chuck.

SAND BEACH COVE   cove, 0.48 km. (0.3 mi.) across, on N coast of Amchitka Island 12.9 km. (8 mi.) SE of Chitka Point; 51°29'10" N, 179°06'40" E. BGN 7504.

SANDY COVE   cove, 0.4 mi. across, in the Aleutian Islands, along the S coast of Amchitka Island 1.3 mi. NW of Buoy Point and 1.8 mi. NE of Windy Island; named for its sand beach, a rarity on the island; 51°34'45" N, 178°50'00" E. BGN 1969.

SASBY ISLAND   island, 0.9 mi. long, in Wrangell Narrows, 1 mi. N of Petersburg; named for John Sasby (1871-1943), a local fisherman who lived in Petersburg; 56°49'45" N, 132°57'00" W. BGN 1970.

SAWMILL CREEK   stream, 0.48 km. (0.3 mi.) long, heads at the junction of its East and West Forks at 61°45'40" N, 149°31'30" W, flows NW to Willow Creek 20.6 km. (12.8 mi.) NNW of Wasilla; Matanuska-Susitna Borough; sec. 6, T 19 N, R 1 W, Seward Mer.; 61°45'47" N, 149°31'58" W. BGN 7902.

Sawmill Creek   stream, see East Fork Sawmill Creek.

SAWTOOTH RANGE	ridge, highest elevation 2,225 m. (7,300 ft.), in the Coast Mountains, 4.8 km. (3 mi.) long, 9.7 km. (6 mi.) NE of Skagway; so named because of the jagged appearance of the peaks on the ridge; T 27 S, Rgs. 60 and 61 E, Copper River Mer.; 59°30'10" N, 135°06'20" W (E end), 59°30'40" N, 135°11'05" W (W end). BGN 8501.
SCHOONER BEACH	beach, 13 km. (8 mi.) long, on NW shore of Yakutat Bay 30 km. (19 mi.) NW of Yakutat; named for a Japanese schooner which was wrecked here about 1900; 59°45'00" N, 140°06'00" W. BGN 7303.
SCIDMORE BAY	bay, 5 mi. long, in Glacier Bay W of the Gilbert Peninsula; 58°48'00" N, 136°37'00" W. BGN 1972.
SCRUB ISLAND	island, in Port Chester 1.1 km. (0.7 mi.) NNE of Metlakatla; T 78 S, R 92 E, Copper River Mer.; 55°08'27" N, 131°34'01" W. Variant: Scrub Islands. BGN 7903.
Scrub Islands	island, see Scrub Island.
Sea Lion Rock	rocks, see Sealion Rocks.
SEA OTTER BAY	bay, 0.81 km. (0.5 mi.) across, on the SE shore of Khantaak Island 4.2 km. (2.7 mi.) NNW of Yakutat; secs. 11, 12, 13, and 14, T 27 S, R 33 E, Copper River Mer.; 59°35'00" N, 139°45'30" W. Variants: Deep Bay. BGN 7702.
SEA OTTER POINT	point of land, in the Aleutian Islands, on the N coast of Amchitka Island 4 mi. SE of Landslide Cove; named for a colony of sea otter which resides here; 51°31'33" N, 179°03'15" E. BGN 1969.
Seagull Island	island, see Gull Island.
Sealion Rock	rocks, see Sealion Rocks.

SEALION ROCKS	rocks, largest 0.81 km. (0.5 mi.) long, in Bering Sea 4 km. (2.5 mi.) NW of Amak Island; translation of the Russian name "Siuchi", derived from the word "Sivuch" meaning "sealion" published by Captain F. P. Lutke, IRN, in 1836; 55°27'40" N, 163°12'00" W. Variants: Sea Lion Rock, Sealion Rock, Siouchi, Sioutchi, Siuchi, Suichi. BGN 7603.
Selenie Lagoon	cove, see Johnson Slough.
SERVICE, MOUNT	peak, elevation 7,847 ft., in the Coast Mountains, on the Alaska-Canada boundary 3.4 mi. SE of Mount Poletica; named for the poet Robert Service; sec. 15, T 32 S, R 65 E, Copper River Mer.; 59°05'23" N, 134°26'47" W. Not: Boundary Peak 101. BGN 1972.
SHADOWS GLACIER	glacier, 8.5 mi. long, heads at 62°25'05" N, 152°40'45" W, trends NNE to the head of an unnamed tributary of the West Fork Yentna River, 9 mi. SSW of Mystic Pass; 62°31'00" N, 152°35'25" W. BGN 1967.
SHADY COVE	cove, 1.3 km. (0.8 mi.) long, on Kenai Peninsula, at W end of Port Nellie Juan 2.1 km. (1.3 mi.) NE of Coxcomb Point; secs. 4 and 5, T 5 N, and secs. 32 and 33, T 6 N, R 6 E, Seward Mer.; 60°33'30" N, 148°25'10" W. BGN 8002.
Shakespeare Peak	peak, see Bard Peak.
SHAKESPEARE SHOULDER	peak, elevation 1,072 m. (3,517 ft.), between Shakespeare and Whittier Glaciers 2.9 km. (1.8 mi.) SW of Whittier; secs. 26 and 27, T 8 N, R 4 E, Seward Mer.; 60°45'12" N, 148°42'46" W. BGN 7702.
SHARKSTOOTH MOUNTAIN	mountain, elevation 8,710 ft., in the Chugach Mountains, 3 mi. NW of Pilot Peak and 30 mi. NW of Valdez; 61°22'01" N, 146°59'15" W. BGN 1965. BGN 1969.
SHATTERED PEAK	peak, elevation 4,202 ft., 5.5 mi. NE of McKinley Peak and 22 mi. W of Cordova; 60°32'00" N, 145°06'20" W. BGN 1967.

Sheep Mountain   mountain, see Langille Mountain.

Sheep Mountain   peaks, see Resurrection Peaks.

SHELF GLACIER   glacier, 4 mi. long, heads at 62°26'05" N, 152°43'10" W, trends N to Shadows Glacier 3.5 mi. SE of Shellabarger Pass; 62°29'15" N, 152°42'50" W. Not: Bench Glacier. BGN 1969.

Shelter Cove   cove, see Hand Trollers Cove.

SHEPHERD MOUNTAINS   mountains, 12.9 km. (8 mi.) long, highest elevation 1,166 m. (3,825 ft.); bound on the E by Shepherd Creek and on the NW by Johns Creek; 46 km. (35 mi.) NNE of Medfra; Tps. 21 and 22 S, Rgs. 23 and 24 E, Kateel River Mer.; 63°40'00" N, 154°14'00" W (NE end), 63°35'30" N, 154°24'00" W (SW end). BGN 8503.

SHIELS, MOUNT   peak, elevation 788 m. (2,585 ft.), in the Heney Range 4 km. (2.5 mi.) SE of Cordova; named for Archibald Williamson Shiels (1878-1974), who worked on the construction of the Copper River and Northwestern Railroad and was the author of several books on Alaska; sec. 35, T 15 S, R 3 W, Copper River Mer.; 60°31'20" N, 145°42'20" W. BGN 7702.

SHIRLEYVILLE   settlement, on Trading Bay 15.3 km. (9.5 mi.) SW of Tyonek; sec. 28, T 11 N, R 12 W, Seward Mer.; 61°00'49" N, 151°24'25" W. BGN 7602.

SHUMAN LAKE   lake, 1.6 km. (1 mi.) long, on the E side of Sheenjek River 16.9 km. (10.5 mi.) NNE of Gailey Lake and 63 km. (39 mi.) NE of Fort Yukon; sec. 28, T 25 N, R 16 E, Fairbanks Mer.; 66°57'42" N, 144°13'45" W. BGN 8301.

SIGNAL COVE   cove, 0.4 mi. long, in the Aleutian Islands, on the S coast of Amchitka Island 7 mi. SE of Aleut Point; named for a World War II building with signal equipment which is located here; 51°35'12" N, 178°45'40" E. BGN 1969.

SILVER SALMON LAKE	lake, 0.5 mi. long, Y-shaped, in the Aleutian Islands, on Amchitka Island 0.5 mi. NW of Stone Beach Cove; this lake is a spawning ground for silver salmon; 51°25'22" N, 179°13'07" E. Not: Pistol Lake. BGN 1969.
SILVERTIP, MOUNT	peak, elevation over 9,400 ft., 8 mi. ESE of the Black Rapids in the Delta River and 32 mi. N of Paxson; 63°29'22" N, 145°36'30" W. Not: Black Warrior Peak, Silvertip Peak. BGN 1968.
Silvertip Peak	peak, see Silvertip, Mount.
Siouchi	rocks, see Sealion Rocks.
Sioutchi	rocks, see Sealion Rocks.
Sioux Glacier	glacier, see Slide Glacier.
SITKOH CREEK	stream, 4 mi. long, on Chichagof Island, heads in Sitkoh Lake at 57°30'50" N, 135°02'30" W, flows E to Sitkoh Bay 36 mi. NNE of Sitka; 57°31'15" N, 134°57'30" W. BGN 1968.
Siuchi	rocks, see Sealion Rocks.
Skeetercake Creek	stream, see Tuluk Creek.
SKI LAKE	lake, 0.2 mi. long, 7 mi. S of Lakeview and 10 mi. N of Seward; 60°15'20" N, 149°21'45" W. BGN 1968.
SKOOKUM GLACIER	glacier, 5 mi. long, in Kenai Mountains, heads at 60°41'10" N, 148°50'30" W, trends NW to its terminus 8 mi. SSE of Portage; 60°44'45" N, 148°55'00" W. BGN 1968.
SKOOKUM GULCH	ravine, 3.2 km. (2 mi.) long, heads 12.9 km. (8 mi.) NNW of Mount Joaquin at 62°58'08" N, 156°19'52" W, trends NW to Yankee Creek valley 16.1 km. (10 mi.) W of Takotna; sec. 6, T 33 N, R 37 W, Seward Mer.; 62°59'05" N, 156°23'00" W. BGN 8402.
SLIDE CREEK	stream, 2.5 mi. long, on Montague Island, heads at 59°50'40" N, 147°42'20" W, flows ESE to Jeanie Cove 3.5 mi. W of Jeanie Point; 59°50'15" N, 147°38'40" W. BGN 1967.

SLIDE GLACIER	glacier, 6 mi. long, heads at 60°32'45" N, 144°13'30" W, trends SW to its terminus 21 mi. NNE of Katalla; 60°29'40" N, 144°18'10" W. Not: Sioux Glacier. BGN 1968.
Slow Mountain Creek	stream, see Little Montana Creek.
SMALL POINT WHITE CREEK	stream, 3.5 km. (2.2 mi.) long, on Kupreanof Island, heads at 56°59'56" N, 133°55'52" W, flows SW to Keku Strait 1.9 km. (1.2 mi.) NW of Kake; sec. 28, T 56 S, R 72 E, Copper River Mer.; 56°59'27" N, 133°57'50" W. BGN 7704.
SMOKE CREEK	stream, 84 km. (52 mi.) long, heads in the Brooks Range at 68°22'07" N, 147°11'00" W, flows SE to the East Fork Chandalar River 35 km. (22 mi.) SW of Arctic Village; North Slope Borough; T 35 N, R 7 E, Fairbanks Mer.; 67°52'40" N, 146°04'00" W. BGN 8203.
SOLF LAKE	lake, 1.6 km. (1 mi.) long, on Knight Island 66 km. (41 mi.) SE of Whittier; named for John D. Solf (1934-1974), Alaska Department of Fish and Game biologist who made numerous contributions to the knowledge of fish biology of Prince William Sound; secs. 16 and 21. T 4 N, R 10 E, Seward Mer.; 60°25'20" N, 147°43'45" W. BGN 7603.
SOUTH FORK YANKEE CREEK	stream, 5.6 km. (3.5 mi.) long, heads 11.3 km. (7 mi.) NNW of Mount Joaquin at 62°57'05" N, 156°19'05" W, flows NW to Yankee Creek 16.9 km. (10.5 mi.) W of Takotna; sec. 1, T 33 N, R 38 W, Seward Mer.; 62°58'18" N, 156°24'08" W. BGN 8402.
Southeast Shoal	shoal, see Tzuse Shoal.
Southeastern Shoal	shoal, see Tzuse Shoal.
SOVEREIGN MOUNTAIN	mountain, elevation 8,849 ft., in the Talkeetna Mountains, on the N side of the head of Talkeetna Glacier 40 mi. NNE of Palmer; 62°07'52" N, 148°36'08" W. Not: Mount Sentry. BGN 1969.

SPENCER PEAK — peak, elevation over 5,800 ft., 13 mi. N of Juneau; named for Arthur Coe Spencer (1871-1964), USGS geologist who was the author of several scientific papers on the Juneau Gold Belt; 58°29'15" N, 134°25'00" W. BGN 1968.

Sphinx Mountain — mountain, see Three Step Mountain.

SPRING CAMP CREEK — stream, 9.2 km. (5.7 mi.) long, heads at 63°45'40" N, 160°37'20" W, flows NW to Norton Sound N of Summer Creek 8 km. (5 mi.) S of Unalakleet; sec. 35, T 19 S, R 11 W, Kateel River Mer.; 63°48'02" N, 160°45'36" W. Not: Taket Creek. BGN 8103.

Spruce Cape — point of land, see Ouzinkie Point.

SPRUCE CREEK — stream, 3.5 mi. long, heads at 57°35'10 N, 133°16'08" W, flows W to Windham Bay at the settlement of Windham; 57°35'40" N, 133°20'08" W. BGN 1969.

Spruce Point — point of land, see Ouzinkie Point.

SQUARE BAY — cove, 0.5 mi. across, on N coast of Amchitka Island 5 mi. NW of Kirilof Point; 51°27'00" N, 179°11'45" W. Not: Cyril Cove. BGN 1973.

STAFANSSON SOUND — lagoon, 54 km. (34 mi.) long, extends SE along the N coast of Alaska from the Return Islands to Newport Entrance and Tigvariak Island; separated from the Beaufort Sea by the Midway Island, Cross Island, and McClure Islands; named for Dr. Vilhjalmar Stefansson (1879-1962), Arctic explorer and leader of many expeditions to North American Arctic coast between 1906 and 1918, including the winter of 1908-1909 on the Colville Delta; 70°27'00" N, 148°33'00" W (NW end), 70°13'00" N, 147°15'00" W (SE end). BGN 7801.

STAMUKHI SHOAL	shoal, 19.3 km. (12 mi.) long, in the Beaufort Sea 17.7 km. (11 mi.) N of the Jones Islands; named for the stamukhi, or stranded fragments of sea ice which mark this shoal; North Slope Borough; 70°45'12" N, 149°33'42" W (NW end), 70°39'42" N, 149°10'12" W (SE end). BGN 7902.
STANEY CONE	mountain, elevation 843 m. (2,765 ft.), on Prince of Wales Island 27 km. (17 mi.) N of Craig; sec. 9, T 71 S, R 80 E, Copper River Mer.; 55°43'43" N, 133°09'12" W. Not: Staneys Cone, Stanley Cone. BGN 7704.
STANEY CREEK	stream, 13 mi. long, on Prince of Wales Island, heads at 55°41'51" N, 132°58'10" W, flows NW to Tuxekan Passage 24 mi. N of Craig; 55°49'12" N, 133°09'15" W. Not: Lester River. 1949. BGN 1967.
STANEY ISLAND	island, 0.64 km. (0.4 mi.) long, in Tuxekan Passage W of mouth of Staney Creek 39 km. (24 mi.) N of Craig; secs. 5, 6, 7, and 8, T 70 S, R 80 E, Copper River Mer.; 55°49'15" N, 133°10'45" W. Not: Staneys Island, Stanley Island. BGN 7704.
Staneys Cone	mountain, see Staney Cone.
Staneys Island	island, see Staney Island.
Stanley Cone	mountain, see Staney Cone.
Stanley Island	island, see Staney Island.
STEELE CREEK	stream, 1.6 km. (1 mi.) long, heads at 60°22'50" N, 144°10'10" W, flows S to an unnamed stream 1.6 km. (1 mi.) W of Kushtaka Lake; sec. 28, T 17 S, R 7 E, Copper River Mer.; 60°22'10" N, 144°10'30" W. BGN 7504.
STONE BEACH COVE	cove, 0.5 mi. across, in the Aleutian Islands, along the N coast of Amchitka Island in the SW end of Kirilof Bay; named for its cobblestone beach; 51°25'00" N, 179°14'00" E. BGN 1969.

STONY POINT   point of land, on the SE coast of Saint
                                     Paul Island in the Pribilof Islands 5
                                     km. (3.1 mi.) NE of the Village of Saint
                                     Paul; 57°08'50" N, 170°12'40" W; 1978
                                     decision revised. Not: Narrow Point,
                                     Rocky Point, Tonki Point (BGN 1978),
                                     Tonkie Mees, Mys Tonkiy. BGN 8103.

STORMY CREEK   stream, 4 km. (2.5 mi.) long, in the
                                     Kenai Mountains, heads at 60°36'40" N,
                                     149°20'13" W, flows WNW to Mills Creek 8
                                     km. (5 mi.) NE of Gilpatricks; Kenai
                                     Peninsula Borough; 60°37'22" N,
                                     149°23'58" W; 1978 description revised.
                                     BGN 8002.

STRAIGHT CREEK   stream, 12.9 km. (8 mi.) long, heads at
                                     69°16'58" N, 145°31'20" W, flows N to
                                     Eagle Creek 14.5 km. (9 mi.) WSW of
                                     Okiotak Peak; sec. 33, T 1 N, R 27 E,
                                     Umiat Mer.; 69°24'03" N, 145°30'55" W.
                                     BGN 7601.

STRAWBERRY ISLAND   island, 0.2 km. (0.1 mi.) long, in
                                     Tenakee Inlet at the E entrance to
                                     Kadashan Bay, off Chicagof Island, 5.6
                                     km. (3.5 mi.) SE of Tenakee Springs;
                                     City and Borough of Sitka; sec. 3, T 48
                                     S, R 63 E, Copper River Mer.; 57°44'20"
                                     N, 135°10'45" W. BGN 8203.

STRICKLAND, MOUNT   mountain, highest elevation 831 km.
                                     (2,725 ft.), on Kodiak Island 35 km. (22
                                     mi.) SE of Karluk; named for Charles W.
                                     Strickland (1935-1983), Refuge Manager
                                     of the Kodiak National Wildlife Refuge;
                                     Kodiak Island Borough; sec. 9, T 33 S, R
                                     30 W, Seward Mer.; 57°20'00" N,
                                     154°03'50" W. BGN 8502.

STRIKE CREEK   stream, 3 mi. long, on Montague island,
                                     heads at 59°50'20" N, 147°43'00" W,
                                     flows SSW to the Gulf of Alaska 2.2 mi.
                                     WNW of Neck Point; 59°48'20" N,
                                     147°44'30" W. BGN 1967.

SUGTUTLIK PEAK   peak, elevation 2,245 ft., S of Amanka
                                     Lake; 59°04'30" N, 159°14'50" W. BGN
                                     1972.

Suichi   rocks, see Sealion Rocks.

Suicide Peak   peaks, see Suicide Peaks.

SUICIDE PEAKS   peaks, higher elevation 1,544 m. (5,065 ft.), in the Chugach Mountains, 24.1 km. (15 mi.) SE of Anchorage; Greater Anchorage Area Borough; sec. 13, 23, and 24, T 11 N, R 2 W, Seward Mer.; 61°02'15" N, 149°33'30" W (N peak), 61°01'45" N, 149°34'22" W (S Peak). Not: Suicide Peak. BGN 8103.

SULLIVAN CREEK   stream, 4.2 mi. long, heads at 64°58'03" N, 145°28'10", flows NW to the East Fork Chena River midway between Palmer and Teuchet Creeks 42 mi. SW of Circle Hot Springs; named for John H. Sullivan (died 1961), pioneer Alaskan who mined in this area for many years; sec. 8, T 2 N, R 11 E, Fairbanks Mer.; 65°00'45" N, 145°33'15" W. BGN 1970.

SUMMER CAMP CREEK   stream, 8 km. (5 mi.) long, heads at 63°42'52" N, 160°39'30" W, flows NE to Norton Sound N of Jesse Creek 12.9 km. (8 mi.) S of Unalakleet; sec. 14, T 20 S, R 11 W, Kateel River Mer.; 63°45'30" N, 160°46'30" W. Not: Coal Mine Creek. BGN 8103.

SUMMIT GLACIER   glacier, 4.8 km. (3 mi.) long, heads at 56°46'00" N, 132°21'45" W, trends NW to end 10.5 km. (6.5 mi.) SE of Simpson Peak; Tps. 58 and 59 S, R 83 E, Copper River Mer.; 56°47'38" N, 132°24'25" W. 1978 description revised. BGN 7902.

SUMMIT LAKE   lake, 2.7 mi. long, in Broad Pass 0.5 mi. SW of Edes Lake and 8 mi. SW of Cantwell; 63°18'15" N, 149°09'30" W; 1927 decision revised. Variant: Lake Edes (former decision). BGN 7303.

SUNNY POINT   point of land, on Chichagof Island, E of Sunshine Cove on the N shore of Tenakee Inlet, 4 km. (2.5 mi.) E of Tenakee Springs; 57°46'36" N, 135°09'03" W. BGN 8203.

SUNSHINE COVE   cove, 0.65 km. (0.4 mi.) across, on Chichagof Island, along the N shore of Tenakee Inlet on W side of Sunny Point, 3.7 km. (2.3 mi.) E of Tenakee Springs; 57°46'45" N, 135°09'15" W. BGN 8203.

SUNSHINE CREEK   stream, 22.5 km. (14 mi.) long, heads in an unnamed lake at 59°29'20" N, 159°20'20" W, flows E through Sunshine Valley to Lake Aleknagik 58 km. (36 mi.) NW of Dillingham; sec. 30, T 8 S, R 57 W, Seward Mer.; 59°27'15" N, 159°02'55" W. BGN 8002.

SUSULATNA HILLS   hills, 9.7 km. (6 mi.) long, highest elevation 890 m. (2,920 ft.), 9.7 km. (6 mi.) NNW of Page Mountain and 59 km. (37 mi.) NW of Medfra; named for the Susulatna River which flows along the W side of the hills; Tps. 22, 23, and 24 S, Rgs. 16 and 17 E, Kateel River Mer.; 63°32'00" N, 155°42'00" W (N end), 63°26'30" N, 155°38'50" W (S end). BGN 8503.

Swanport   locality, see Dayville.

Sweetheart Lake   lake, see Lower Sweetheart Lake.

SWIFT CREEK   stream, 4 km. (2.5 mi.) long, heads at 64°25'33" N, 155°34'30" W, flows SE to Basin Creek 39 km. (24 mi.) S of Ruby; sec. 35, T 12 S, R 16 E, Kateel River Mer.; 64°24'01" N, 155°36'35" W; 1936 decision revised. Not: Willow Creek (former decision). BGN 7704.

Swift Creek   stream, see Lion Creek.

SWITZER CREEK   stream, 1.3 mi. long, heads at 58°22'30" N, 134°30'30" W, flows S to the Gastineau Channel 5 mi. NW of Juneau; 58°21'42" N, 134°30'13" W. BGN 1968.

SYMPHONY LAKE   lake, 0.5 mi. long, in Chugach Mountains 17 mi. E of Anchorage; 61°10'30" N, 149°22'45" W. BGN 1968.

TAAN FIORD	fiord, 8 km. (5 mi.) long on E side of Icy Bay 22 km. (14 mi.) NNE of Point Riou; exposed by recent retreat of Tyndall Glacier,, 60°04'15" N, 141°20'00" W. BGN 7303.
Taiya	locality, see Dyea.
Taket Creek	stream, see Spring Camp Creek.
Tananak	village, see Tununak.
Tanuna	village, see Tununak.
Tanunak	village, see Tununak.
Tanunak Bay	bay, see Tununak Bay.
Tanunak River	stream, see Tununak.
Tanurah	village, see Tununak.
Tapkaluk Island	island, see Tapkaluk Islands.
TAPKALUK ISLANDS	islands, 9 mi. long, on the Beaufort Sea coast, 7 mi. SE of Point Barrow and 14 mi. ENE of Barrow; 71°19' N, 156°01' W. Not: Deadmans Island, Tapkaluk Island. 1919. BGN 1967.
TATINA GLACIER	glacier, 6 mi. long, heads at 62°24'20" N, 152°46'10" W, trends NNW to head of the Tatina River 8 mi. NW of Lewis Peak; 62°29'10" N, 152°50'00" W. BGN 1967.
TEAL CREEK	stream, 2 mi. long, in the Aleutian Islands, heads at 51°29'05" N, 179°04'32" E, flows SW to the Pacific Ocean on the S coast of Amchitka Island; named for the ducks found in abundance here; 51°28'07" N, 179°03'21" E. BGN 1969.
Televak Inlet	water passage, see Klawock Inlet.
TELSITNA RIDGE	ridge, 12.9 km. (8 mi.) long, highest elevation 1,036 m. (3,400 ft.), 8 km. (5 mi.) SW of Novi Mountain and 100 km. (62 mi.) NE of Medfra; named for the Telsitna River which heads on the NW side of the ridge; Tps. 17, 18, and 19 S, Rgs. 26 and 27 E, Kateel River Mer.; 63°58'20" N, 153°36'00" W (NE end), 63°52'00" N, 153°43'00" W (SW end). BGN 8503.

TERN LAKE	lake, 0.7 mi. long, on Kenai Peninsula, 4 mi. NW of Upper Trail Lake and 5 mi. S of Gilpatricks; 60°32'00" N, 149°32'45" W. Not: Mud Lake. 1963. BGN 1967.
TEVYARAQ LAKE	lake, 2.9 km. (1.8 mi.) long and 0.48 km. (0.3 mi.) wide, in the Kiokluk Mountains 66 km. (41 mi.) SW of Sleetmute; Upik Eskimo word for "portage" or "to go over something"; secs. 2 and 3, T 13 N, and secs. 26, 27, 34, and 35, T 14 N, R 49 W, Seward Mer.; 61°16'05" N, 158°01'50" W. Not: Kiokluk Lake. BGN 8302.
The Sphinx	mountain, see Face Mountain.
THIBODEAUX MOUNTAIN	mountain, elevation 7,620 ft., in the Brooks Range 20 mi. ENE of Marshmallow Mountain; named for Jules Thibodeaux, a French-Eskimo bush pilot who crashed in the area of this peak in 1965; 68°17'15" N, 150°05'50" W. BGN 1969.
THOR, MOUNT	mountain, highest elevation 12,500 ft., in the Chugach Mountains 3 mi. NW of Mount Valhalla; named for Thor, the Norse God of Thunder, because of the noise of avalanches on the mountain; 61°29'08" N, 147°08'32" W. Not: Mount Willard Gibbs. BGN 1969.
THREE STEP MOUNTAIN	mountain, elevation 301 m. (989 ft.), between the Kwethluk and Akulikutak Rivers, 47 km. (29 mi.) SE of Bethel; so named because the mountain has three definite benches; T 5 N, R 67 W, Seward Mer.; 60°32'40" N, 161°05'05" W; 1978 description revised. Not: Flattop Mountain, Sphinx Mountain. BGN 8102.
THUMB POINTS	point of land, on Prince of Wales Island, extends NW into McKenzie Inlet 47 km. (29 mi.) WNW of Ketchikan; point resembles the thumb of a mitten; secs. 5 and 8, T 75 S, R 86 E, Copper River Mer.; 55°23'30" N, 132°22'00" W. BGN 7902.

THUNDER BIRD PEAK	peak, elevation 6,575 ft., at the head of Thunder Bird Creek 3 mi. WSW of the S end of Eklutna Lake and 28 mi. ENE of Anchorage; sec. 9, T 14 N, R 2 E, Seward Mer.; 61°19'10" N, 149°05'24" W. BGN 1971.
THUNDER MOUNTAIN	mountain, elevation 2,900 ft., at the SW end of Heintzleman Ridge 6.8 mi. NW of Juneau; 58°22'53" N, 134°31'30" W. 1965. BGN 1968.
TIBUKLIGARRA	creek, Seward Peninsula, a tributary to the Inglutalik River from the west, 65°00' N, 160°00' W. VACATED. 1907. BGN 1966.
TIGARA PENINSULA	peninsula, on the Lisburne Peninsula, extends W (from 166°18' W) 21 km. (13 mi.) into the Chukchi Sea to terminate at Point Hope; Eskimo name meaning "forefinger"; 68°21'00" N, 166°30'00" W. BGN 7402.
Tikikluk	village, see Atqasuk.
Tikilook	village, see Atqasuk.
Tikiluk	village, see Atqasuk.
TIMBER POINT	point of land, in Le Conte Bay 2.9 km. (1.8 mi.) NE of Indian Point and 29 km. (18 mi.) SE of Petersburg; sec. 10, T 59 S, R 82 E, Copper River Mer.; 56°46'10" N, 132°29'15" W. BGN 7702.
TINCAN PEAK	peak, elevation over 4,400 ft., in the Kenai Mountains 8 mi. SW of Portage; 60°44'22" N, 149°05'40" W. 1912. BGN 1968.
TLA-XAGH ISLAND	island, 0.64 km. (0.4 mi.) long, in Yakutat Bay 20.9 km. (13 mi.) NE of Yakutat; secs. 32 and 33, T 25 S, R 35 E, Copper River Mer.; 59°42'03" N, 139°30'10" W. Variant: Eleanor Island. BGN 7702.
Tlevakh Inlet	water passage, see Klawock Inlet.
Tlevakkhyn Bay	water passage, see Klawock Inlet.

TOLSTOI LAKE	lake, 1.6 km. (1 mi.) long, 16.9 km. (10.5 mi.) NNW of Crater Mountain and 32 km. (20 mi.) SW of Ophir; secs. 7 and 18, T 33 N, R 40 W, Seward Mer. 62°57'15" N, 156°56'00" W. BGN 8402.
TONALITE CREEK	stream, 13.5 km. (8.4 mi.) long, heads at 57°35'10" N, 135°14'15" W, flows N to the Kadashan River 1.3 km. (0.8 mi.) S of Kadashan Bay and 72 km. (45 mi.) N of Sitka; Sitka Borough; sec. 21, T 48 S, R 63 E, Copper River Mer.; 57°41'41" N, 135°13'00" W. Not: Hook Creek. BGN 8301.
Tonki Point	point of land, see Stony Point.
Tonkie Mees	point of land, see Stony Point.
Tonkina River	stream, see Gulkana River.
Toolemina Island	island, see Tulimanik Island.
Toolik Lake	lake, see Itigaknit Lake.
Toolook Creek	stream, see Tuluk Creek.
TORTUOUS CREEK	stream, 2.5 mi. long, on Montague Island, heads at 59°51'45" N, 147°40'20" W, flows SE to Jeanie Cove 3 mi. WNW of Jeanie Point; 59°50'40" N, 147°37'50" W. BGN 1967.
TOTEM BIGHT	bight, 0.7 mi. wide, on the SW coast of Revillagigedo Island, 8 mi. NW of Ketchikan; 55°25'20" N, 131°46'20" W. 1954. BGN 1968.
TOTUCK LAKE	lake, 0.32 km. (0.2 mi.) long, one of the Meadow Lakes located N of Island Lake 11 km. (6.8 mi.) NW of Wasilla; Matanuska-Susitna Borough; sec. 22, T 18 N, R 2 W, Seward Mer.; 61°38'07" N, 149°36'37" W. BGN 8002.
TRIANGLE PEAK	peak, elevation 5,375 ft., at the head of Mendenhall Glacier 2.4 mi. WSW of Snowdrift Peak and 19 mi. NNW of Juneau; the name is descriptive; sec. 16, T 38 S, R 66 E, Copper River Mer.; 58°34'20" N, 134°30'55" W. BGN 1971.

Trident, The — mountain, see Trident Volcano.

TRIDENT VOLCANO — mountain, 3 mi. across, in Katmai National Monument, between a glacier on the E and Katmai Pass on the W, 5 mi. SW of Mount Katmai; 58°14' N, 155°06' W (center). Not: Mount Trident (former decision), The Trident. BGN 1966. BGN 1968.

TRINITY LAKE — lake, 2.4 mi. long and 0.2 mi. wide, larger and more southern lake of the Trinity Lakes, 9 mi. SW of Beluga Mountain; 61°36' N, 151°27' W. BGN 1967.

TRUULI CREEK — stream, 6 mi. long, heads at the terminus of Truuli Glacier at 59°57'55" N, 150°30'20" W, flows N to Tustumena Glacier 3.5 mi. SE of Tustumena Lake; 60°02'10" N, 150°33'40" W. BGN 1969.

TRUULI GLACIER — glacier, 5 mi. long, heads 1 mi. NE of Truuli Peak at 59°55'10" N, 150°23'15" W, trends NW to the head of Truuli Creek 7 mi. SE of Tustumena Lake; 59°57'55" N, 150°30'20" W. BGN 1969.

TSAA FIORD — fiord, 5.5 km. (3.5 mi.) long, on W side of Icy Bay 21 km. (13.5 mi.) N of Point Riou; exposed by recent retreat of Guyot Glacier; 60°04'30" N, 141°26'30" W. BGN 7303.

Tschigmit Gebirge — mountains, see Chigmit Mountains.

TSIMPSHIAN POINT — point of land, on Point Riou Spit 5.5 km. (3.4 mi.) WSW of Moraine Island; T 23 S, R 23 E, Copper River Mer.; 59°54'50" N, 141°28'46" W. Not: Crested Point (BGN 1978). BGN 8001.

Tsumianug Creek — stream, see Whakatna Creek.

Tuklukyet — village, see Nukluklayet.

TUKMAKNA — creek, Matanaska Valley, tributary of Mudflow Creek, flowing SW and entering it near 61°49'30" N, 148°06'00" W. VACATED. BGN 1932. BGN 1966.

TULCAN SLOUGH	cove, 0.64 km. (0.4 mi.) long, on the S shore of Port Graham, 0.8 km. (0.5 mi.) E of Duncan Slough and 1.6 km. (1 mi.) SE of the village of Port Graham; Kenai Peninsula Borough; secs. 3 and 4, T 10 S, R 15 W, Seward Mer.; 59°20'40" N, 151°48'30" W. BGN 8203.
Tulimanak Island	island, see Tulimanik Island.
TULIMANIK ISLAND	island, 1.3 mi. long, on the NE side of Fatigue Bay, 3 mi. ESE of Tangent Point and 44 mi. ESE of Barrow; 71°07'45" N, 154°57'00" W. Not: Toolemina Island, Tulimanak Island, Tullimanirk Island, Tulmanik Island. 1854. BGN 1967.
Tullimanirk Island	island, see Tulimanik Island.
Tulmanik Island	island, see Tulimanik Island.
TULUK CREEK	stream, 40 km. (25 mi.) long, heads at 69°20'47" N, 148°46'55" W, flows NNW to Toolik River 129 km. (80 mi.) ENE of Umiat; sec. 21, T 3 N, R 13 E, Umiat Mer.; 69°35'56" N, 148°56'50" W. Not: Skeetercake Creek, Tuluq Creek, Toolook Creek. BGN 7903.
Tuluq Creek	stream, see Tuluk Creek.
TUNGAK LAKE	lake, 2.2 km. (1.4 mi.) long at NW edge of the Ingakslugwat Hills 32 km. (20 mi.) NW of Chakwaktolik; Eskimo word meaning "shaman" or "medicine man"; secs. 4 and 5, T 5 N, and secs. 32 and 33, T 16 N, R 83 W, Seward Mer.; 61°25'40" N, 164°11'30" W. BGN 8002.
Tununa	village, see Tununak.
TUNUNAK	village, on Nelson Island 9.7 km. (6 mi.) NE of Cape Vancouver; sec. 28, T 6 N, R 91 W, Seward Mer.; 60°35'07" N, 165°15'20" W. Variants: Dununak, Dununuk, Tananak, Tanuna, Tanunah, Tanunak, Tununa, Tununuk. BGN 7603.
TUNUNAK BAY	bay, 7.2 km. (4.5 mi.) long, on Nelson Island 5.6 km. (3.5 mi.) NE of Cape Vancouver; T 6 N, Rgs. 91 and 92 W, Seward Mer.; 60°35'15" N, 165°18'00" W. Variant: Tanunak Bay. BGN 7603.

TUNUNAK RIVER	stream, 11.3 km. (7 mi.) long, heads at 60°30'45" N, 165°17'30" W, flows N to Tununak Bay SW of Tununak; sec. 29, T 6 N, R 91 W, Seward Mer.; 60°34'42" N, 165°16'10" W. Variant: Tanunak River. BGN 7603.
Tununuk	village, see Tununak.
TURNAGAIN PASS	pass, between the heads of Granite and Ingram Creeks. 6 mi. S of Turnagain Arm and 18 mi. WNW of Whittier; 60°48'10" N, 149°11'20" W. Not: Johnson Pass. BGN 1968.
TWAHARPIES GLACIER	glacier, 13 mi. long, heads in the University Range at 61°22'15" N, 141°58'45" W, trends W to the head of Glacier Creek, 18 mi. WNW of University Peak and 22 mi. E of McCarthy; 61°24'28" N, 142°17'30" W. BGN 1967.
TWAHARPIES, THE	peaks, group of three, highest elevation 14,445 ft., in the University Range between the heads of Hawkins and Twaharpies Glaciers; the peaks are named Aello, Celeno, and Ocypete; 61°20'30" N, 141°56'30" W. BGN 1967.
TWIN HILLS	populated place, on SE bank of an E distributary of the Togiak River 5.9 km. (3.7 mi.) NE of Togiak; Bristol Bay Borough; secs. 3 and 4, T 13 S, R 66 W, Seward Mer.; 59°04'45" N, 160°16'30" W. BGN 8002.
TWIN ROCKS	rocks, in Resurrection Bay off the E coast of the Kenai Peninsula 4.8 km. (3 mi.) NNE of Callisto Head; Kenai Peninsula Borough; sec. 34, T 2 S, R 1 W, Seward Mer.; 59°57'36" N, 149°26'15" W. BGN 8003.
TYNDALL GLACIER	glacier, 22 km. (14 mi.) long, heads at 60°15'10" N, 141°06'00" W, on SW slope of Saint Elias Mountains, trends SW to Taan Fiord 27 km. (17 mi.) NNE of Point Riou; named for John Tyndall (1820-1893), British physicist, natural philosopher, and glaciologist; 60°05'45" N, 141°14'10" W. BGN 7303.

Tyya	locality, see Dyea.

TZUSE SHOAL	shoal, 0.64 km. (0.4 mi.) long, at S entrance to Yakutat Roads, N of Monti Bay and 2.2 km. (1.4 mi.) NW of Yakutat; 59°33'40" N, 139°45'55" W. Variants: Eastern Shoal, Southeastern Shoal, Southeast Shoal. BGN 7702.

Ultima Peak	peak, see Parka Peak.
ULTRA CREEK	stream, 1.5 mi. long, in the Aleutian Islands, heads at 51°26'44"N, 179°07'45" E, flows SW to the Pacific Ocean on the S coast of Amchitka Island 3.8 mi. NW of Rifle Range Point; named for the basin which it drains; 51°26'07" N, 179°06'25" E. BGN 1969.
UNGALIKTHLUK BAY	bay, 4.5 km. (2.8 mi.) across, on N shore of Bristol Bay, at the mouth of the Ungalikthluk River 2.7 km (1.7 mi.) NNE of Summit Island; 58°53'00" N, 160°11'00" W. BGN 8504.
Unzinki Narrows	water passage, see Ouzinkie Narrows.
Upper Bonnie Lake	lake, see June Biffle Lake.
UPPER SWEETHEART LAKE	lake, 1.5 mi. long, 13 mi. N of Mount Sumdum and 38 mi. SE of Juneau; 57°59'45" N, 133°29'30" W. 1955. BGN 1967.
Uzinki Narrows	water passage, see Ouzinkie Narrows.
Uzinki Point	point of land, see Ouzinkie Point.

Valdes						populated place, see Old Valdez.

VALDEZ						populated place, (incorporated city), on N shore of Port Valdez; Twps. 8 and 9 S, R 6 W, Copper River Mer.; 61°08'00" N, 146°21'00" W; 1978 decision revised. Not: Copper City, Old Valdez (BGN 1978). BGN 8003.

VOLKMAR LAKE				lake, 1.5 mi. across, 3 mi. N of the Tanana River and 18 mi. E of Big Delta; 64°07'30" N, 145°10'30" W. Not: Magoffin Lake. 1887. BGN 1967.

WALATKA MOUNTAINS   mountains, highest elevation 4,625 ft., in the Aleutian Range 35 mi. N of Mount Katmai; named for John Walatka, pioneer Alaska bush pilot, who for many years served the communities of the Alaska Peninsula; 58°47'25" N, 155°02'00" W (S end), 59°00'50" N, 154°50'10" W (N end). BGN 7304.

WARBELOW, MOUNT   mountain, highest elevation 5,553 ft., 14 mi. NW of the village of Chicken, named for Marvin E. Warbelow (1917-1971), a local bush pilot; 64°14'50" N, 142°09'40" W. BGN 1972.

WASHINGTON MONUMENT ROCK   rock, submerged, in Thorne Arm near Revillagigedo Channel 4 km. (2.5 mi.) E of Bold Island and 24 km. (14.9 mi.) SE of Ketchikan; 55°14'28" N, 131°20'23" W; 1978 description revised. BGN 8102.

WAW, MOUNT   mountain, elevation 2,626 m. (8,615 ft.), in the Romanzof Mountains, 4.3 km. (2.7 mi.) N of Mount Hubley and 19.3 km. (12 mi.) E of Mount Michelson; sec. 36, T 1 S, R 34 E, Umiat Mer.; 69°18'50" N, 143°47'30" W. BGN 7902.

WAYNE TAYLOR PEAK   peak, elevation 1,092 m. (3,581 ft.), in the Taylor Mountains 90 km. (56 mi.) S of Sleetmute; named for A. Wayne Taylor (1951-1979), Alaska Bush pilot; sec. 27, T 10 N, R 46 W, Seward Mer.; 60°55'30" N, 157°24'22" W. BGN 8301.

WEATHER RIDGE   ridge, 13 mi. long, highest elevation 2,100 ft., 30 mi. SE of Candle; name derived from its barrier-effect arresting storms from the west; 65°33'45" N, 161°34'30" W (NW end), 65°25'00" N, 161°22'00" W (SE end). BGN 1969.

WEBSTER, POINT   point of land, on SW coast of Prince of Wales Island 29 km. (18 mi.) SE of Hydaburg; sec. 33, T 79 S, R 85 E, Copper River Mer.; 54°58'15" N, 132°36'45" W. Variant: Webster Point. BGN 7702.

WELLER CREEK	stream, 6.4 km. (4 mi.) long, heads at 69°38'30" N, 144°52'42" W, flows E to Itkilyariak Creek 6.4 km. (4 mi.) E of Mount Weller; named for Mount Weller; sec. 3, T 3 N, R 30 E, Umiat Mer.; 69°38'55" N, 144°43'10" W. BGN 7504.
WEST ALAPAH GLACIER	glacier, 2 mi. long, heads on Alapah Mountain at 68°07'50" N, 150°51'30" W, trends N to the head of Alapah Creek 5 mi. W of Cockedhat Mountain; 68°09'30" N, 150°52'00" W. BGN 1969.
WEST BUTTERFLY LAKE	lake, 0.5 mi. across, W of East Butterfly Lake and 27 mi. NW of Anchorage; 61°35'25" N, 150°08'15" W. Not: Butterfly Lake, Delyndia Lake. BGN 1968.
West Butterfly Lake	lake, see Butterfly Lake.
WEST CREEK	stream, 8.4 km. (5.2 mi.) long, heads at 57°52'20" N, 155°22'20" W, flows E to Bear Bay 7.7 km. (4.8 mi.) WSW of Mount Kubugakli and 56 km. (35 mi.) NW of Karluk; sec. 7, T 27 S, R 36 W, Seward Mer.; 57°51'45" N, 155°15'15" W. BGN 8401.
WEST FINGER INLET	inlet, 4 km. (2.5 mi.) long, on Kenai Peninsula, opens into Kings Bay 3.2 km. (2 mi.) N of Coxcomb Point; secs. 21, 28, 29, and 32, T 6 N, R 6 E, Seward Mer.; 60°34'00" N, 148°26'30" W. BGN 8002.
WEST FORK MARSH CREEK	stream, 12.9 km. (8 mi.) long, heads at 69°43'23" N, 145°00'30" W, flows NE of Marsh Creek 19.3 km. (12 mi.) S of Collinson Point; sec. 3, T 5 N, R 29 E, Umiat Mer.; 69°49'25" N, 144°51'00" W. BGN 7504.
WEST FORK SAWMILL CREEK	stream, 2.7 km. (1.7 mi.) long, heads at 61°44'08" N, 149°31'50" W, flows N to join the East Fork to form Sawmill Creek 20.1 km. (12.5 mi.) NNW of Wasilla; Matanuska-Susitna Borough; sec. 6, T 19 N, R 1 W, Seward Mer.; 61°45'40" N, 149°31'30" W. BGN 7902.

WEST NULARVIK CREEK   stream, 1.6 km. (1mi.) long, heads at 69°38'10" N, 145°06'25" W, flows E to the Nularvik River 6.4 km. (4 mi.) W of Mount Weller; sec. 5, T 3 N, R 29 E, Umiat Mer.; 69°38'15" N, 145°03'55" W. BGN 7501.

WEST PHELAN CREEK   stream, 2.5 mi. long, heads at West Gulkana Glacier at 63°15'30" N, 145°29'30" W, flows S to Phelan Creek 13 mi. N of Paxson; 63°13'35" N, 145°29'05" W. BGN 1969.

WEST POINT SHOAL   shoal, in Cook Inlet, 2.2 km. (1.4 mi.) NW of West Point on Fire Island 24.1 km. (15 mi.) SW of Anchorage; Municipality of Anchorage; 61°08'35" N, 150°18'42" W. BGN 8501.

WEST REDCLIFF ISLAND   island, 0.8 km. (0.5 mi.) long, one of the Redcliff Islands in Freshwater Bay 14.5 km. (9 mi.) NE of the village of Tenakee Springs; 57°53'55" N, 135°06'30" W. BGN 8103.

WESTDAHL POINT   point of land, in Muir Inlet 3 mi. N of Wachusett Inlet; named for the USC&GS vessel _Westdahl_, which was engaged in charting Muir Inlet in 1933 and 1940; 58°58'45" N, 136°08'30" W. Not: Arcadia Point. 1941. BGN 1972.

WESTERN CHANNEL   water passage, 3.7 km. (2.3 mi.) long, extends S between Hawkins and Observation Islands from Orca Channel at Salmo Point to Odiak Channel 3 mi. N of Cordova; secs. 33 and 34, T 14 S, and secs. 3, 4, 9, and 10, T 15 S, R 3 W, Copper River Mer.; 60°37'00" N, 145°45'00" W (N end), 60°35'00" N, 145°45'30" W (S end). Variant: Odiak Channel. BGN 7402.

WEYAHOK RIVER   stream, 16.1 km. (10 mi.) long, heads at 67°46'15" N, 115°22'30" W, flows NE to Alatna River 48 km. (30 mi.) N of Mount Igikpak, named for Howard Rock, Eskimo name "Weyahok", (1911-1976), artist, editor of the _Tundra Times_ and 1974 Alaskan Man of the Year; T 28 N, R 17 E, Kateel River Mer.; 67°50'10" N, 155°07'30" W. BGN 7801.

WHAKATNA CREEK   stream, 88 km. (55 mi.) long, heads at 64°55'48" N, 155°44'15" W, flows WNW to Bear Creek 16.1 km. (10 mi.) N of Galena; sec. 23, T 7 S, R 9 E, Kateel River Mer.; 64°52'20" N, 156°58'28" W. Not: Bear Creek, Tsumianug Creek, Whatkatena Creek, Zumianug Creek. BGN 7704.

WHALE COVE   cove, 0.4 mi. across, in the Aleutian Islands, on the N coast of Amchitka Island, just E of Constantine Point and 1.7 mi. SW of Ivakin Point; named for whale sighted here; 51°24'18" N, 179°21'20" E. BGN 1969.

WHALE MOUNTAIN   mountain, 16.9 km. (10.5 mi.) long, 64 km. (40 mi.) SE of Egegik; named for the whale-like appearance of this feature as seen from the surface of Beeharof Lake; Tps. 23, 24, and 25 S, Rgs. 43, 44, and 45 W, Seward Mer.; 58°08'05" N, 156°34'20" W (NW end), 58°02'40" N, 156°20'20" W (SE end). Variant: Blue Mountain. BGN 7504.

Whale Point   point of land, see Kitovi Point.

Whatkatena Creek   stream, see Whakatna Creek.

WHISTLING LAKE   lake, 0.7 mi. long and 0.3 mi. wide, 1.6 mi. NE of Amber Lake and 14 mi. SW of Talkeetna; named for the whistling swans which nest and raise their young here; sec. 1, T 24 N, R 7 W, Seward Mer.; 62°11'45" N, 150°28'30" W. BGN 1970.

WHITE ALICE CREEK   stream, 2 mi. long, in the Aleutian Islands, heads at 51°28'24" N, 179°05'42" E, flows ENE to the Bering Sea on the N coast of Amchitka Island 0.4 mi. W of Banjo Point; named for a communications site once located here. 51°28'45" N, 179°07'38" E. BGN 1969.

Whitsol Lake   lake, see Witsoe Lake.

WILBUR, MOUNT   mountain, elevation 10,821 ft., in Glacier Bay National Monument, in the Fairweather Range 1.3 mi. W of Mount Orville and 8 mi. NW of Mount Crillon; named for Wilbur Wright (1867-1912), who, with his brother Orville, invented the airplane, the form of transportation that has contributed greatly to the development of Alaska; 58°44'25" N, 137°19'00" W. BGN 1962. BGN 1967.

WILDWOOD   locality, on W side of Kenai Peninsula, 4 km. (2.5 mi.) NW of Kenai; sec. 25, T 6 N, R 12 W, Seward Mer.; 60°35'00" N, 151°18'00" W. Not: Wildwood Air Force Station, Wildwood Station. BGN 7904.

Wildwood Air Force Station   locality, see Wildwood.

Wildwood Station   locality, see Wildwood.

WILLARD GLACIER   glacier,, 3 mi. long, heads on N slope of Takhinsha Mountains, trends N to its terminus 1 mi. S of the Takhin River and 15 mi. W of Haines; named for Rev. Eugene S. Willard, missionary to the Chilkat Indians near Haines in 1881-82; 59°14' N, 135°52' W. BGN 1967.

WILLIAM HENRY CREEK   stream, 3 mi. long, heads at 58°44'00" N, 135°18'58" W, flows E to William Henry Bay 42 mi. NW of Juneau; 58°43'30" N, 135°14'20" W. BGN 1968.

WILLOW CREEK   stream, 4 km. (2.5 mi.) long, heads at 64°24'27" N, 155°33'25" W, flows SW to Basin Creek 40 km. (25 mi.) S of Ruby; sec. 1, T 13 S, R 16 E, Kateel River Mer.; 64°23'08" N, 155°37'25" W. BGN 7704.

Willow Creek   stream, see Swift Creek.

WILLOW LAKE   lake, 4.8 km. (3 mi.) across, 7.2 km. (4.5 mi.) SSE of Boat Lake and 16.1 km. (10 mi.) E of Huslia; Tps. 3 and 4 N, Rgs. 13 and 14 E, Kateel River Mer.; 65°41'45" N, 156°04'00" W. Not: Boat Lake. BGN 8202.

WINDY ISLAND   island, 0.3 mi. long, in the Aleutian Islands, 0.15 mi. off the S coast of Amchitka Island and 8.7 mi. SE of Aleut Point; the island is exposed to strong SW winds; 51°34'05" N, 178°47'18" E. BGN 1969.

WITSOE LAKE   lake, 1.6 km. (1 mi.) long, 16.9 km. (10.5 mi.) N of Susitna; named for Hank Witsoe, who with his family hunted in this area; secs. 34 and 35, T 19 N, R 7 W, Seward Mer.; 61°41'40" N, 150°30'10" W. Variant: Whitsol Lake. BGN 7503.

WOLF CREEK   stream, 6 mi. long, heads at 55°30'15" N, 131°35'30" W, flows NNW through Upper and Lower Wolf Lakes to Moser Bay, 15 mi. N of Ketchikan; 55°33'35" N, 131°39'00" W. BGN 1968.

WOLVERINE CREEK   stream, 2 mi. long, heads at the terminus of Wolverine Glacier, flows SSE to the Nellie Juan River 8.5 mi. NE of Nellie Juan Lake; 60°21'10" N, 148°52'50" W. BGN 1969.

WOLVERINE GLACIER   glacier, 5 mi. long, heads at 60°26'10" N, 148°54'00" W, trends S to the head of Wolverine Creek 9 mi. SW of Kings Bay; 60°22'15" N, 148°53'50" W. BGN 1969.

WOOLFE FORK   stream, 17 mi. long, heads at 68°25'30" N, 163°50'20" W, flows NW to Ipewik River 8 mi. SE of Windy Lake; named for Henry D. Woolfe, who travelled through and reported on this area in the late 1800's; sec. 20, T 10 S, R 52 W, Umiat Mer.; 68°33'40" N, 164°07'10" W. BGN 1972.

WORONZOF SHOAL   shoal, 5.6 km. (3.5 mi.) long, in Knik Arm, between Fire Island and Point Woronzof, 8 km. (5 mi.) WSW of Anchorage, Anchorage Bor.; 61°12'10" N, 150°02'00" W (NE end), 61°11'07" N, 150°07'44" W (SW end). BGN 8402.

WRATHER, MOUNT   mountain, elevation 5,968 ft., 13 mi. N of Juneau; named for William Embry Wrather (1883-1963), Director of the U.S. Geological Survey from 1943 to 1956; 58°29'25" N, 134°28'50" W. BGN 1968.

WRONG MOUNTAIN   mountain, elevation 1,603 m. (5,260 ft.), 4.8 km. (3 mi.) N of Crescent Lake and 42 km. (26 mi.) N of Seward; sec. 30, T 5 N, R 1 W, Seward Mer.; 60°29'30" N, 149°31'30" W. BGN 7802.

Yelovoi point of land, see Ouzinkie Point.

YENSUS LAKE lake, 0.7 mi. long, 3.2 mi. NW of Susitna; name derived from the nearby Yentna and Susitna Rivers; secs. 7, 8, 17, and 18, T 17 N, R 7 W, Seward Mer.; 61°34'25" N, 150°35'00" W. BGN 1972.

ZAGOSKIN LAKE	lake, 0.48 km. (0.3 mi.) wide, on Saint Michael Island 4.8 km. (3 mi.) SW of Saint Michael; named for Lieutenant Laurenti Alexief Zagoskin, Russian naval officer who explored and surveyed this area in 1842-1844; secs. 34 and 35, T 23 S, R 18 W, Kateel River Mer.; 63°26'56" N, 162°06'25" W. BGN 8002.
Zaliv Tlevakkhan	water passage, see Klawock Inlet.
ZIMOVIA STRAIT	water passage, extends 30 mi. NW from Ernest Sound, between Wrangell Island on the E and Etolin and Woronkofski Islands on the W; 56°27'50" N, 132°26'30" W (NW end), 56°06'35" N, 132°05'15" W (SE end). Not: Proliv Zimovya. 1853. BGN 1968.
Zumianug Creek	stream, see Whakatna Creek.

INDEX

Alaska, Chamber of Commerce	see, Clarence Kramer Peak.
Alaska, Commissioner of Mines	see, Ben Stewart, Mount.
Alaska, Department of Fish and Game	see, Jonathan Ward, Mount; Solf Lake
Alaska, Department of Health and Social Services	see, Manty Mountain.
Alaska, Governor	see, Ernest Gruening, Mount.
Alaska, Legislature	see, Foster, Mount.
Alaska Northern Railroad	see, Lakeside.
Alaska, Office of Air Commerce	see, Foster, Mount.
Alaska, Senate	see, L V Ray Peak.
Alaska Sportsman	see, Emery Tobin, Lake.
Alaska, Territorial Mine Inspector	see, Ben Stewart, Mount.
Alaska Weekly	see, Lulu Fairbanks, Mount.
Alaskan Engineering Commission	see, Edes Lake.
Aleyska Ski Resort	see, Baumann Bump.
Anderson, Paul	see, Anderson Peak.
Arctic Institute of North America	see, Foresta, Mount.
Balchen, Bernt	see, Balchen, Mount.
Baldwin, George Clyde	see, Baldwin, Mount.
Bartlett, Sen. Edward Lewis (Bob)	see, Bartlett Hills.
Bartlett, Capt. Robert Abram	see, Bartlett Island.
Baumann, Ernst	see, Baumann Bump.
Begich, Cong. Nicholas	see, Begich Peak; Boggs Peak.
Benson, Bennie	see, Benson, Mount.
Bering, Vitus	see, Saint Makarius Point.
Besser, William	see, Bill Besser Lake.
Biffle, June	see, June Biffle Lake.
Biffle, Roy	see, June Biffle Lake.
Blackburn, Louis	see, French Joe Mountain.
Blankenship, Walter R.	see, Blankenship Creek.
Bocharov, Dimitrii Ivanovich	see, Bocharov Island; Izmaylov Island.
Boggs, Cong. Thomas Hale	see, Begich Peak; Boggs Peak.
Brackett, George	see, Brackett, Mount.
Bradley, Lois I.	see, Bradley Peak.
Brock, R. W.	see, Brock, Mount.
Chapin, Theodore S.	see, Chapin Peak.
Cook, Capt. James	see, Ledyard Bay.
Cooper, Dr. William Skinner	see, Cooper, Mount.
Cravens, Larry Frank	see, Cravens Peak.
Culver, Don	see, Longmere Lake.
Dalton, James	see, James Dalton Mountain.
Dickinson, George	see, Dickinson Glacier.
Douglass, Chief	see, Douglass Island.
Edes, William C.	see, Edes Lake.
Elliot, H. W.	see, Kitovi Point.
Ellison, Jr., Carl Oscar	see, Ellison, Mount.
Eskilida Family	see, Eskilida Creek.

Fairbanks, Lulu	see, Lulu Fairbanks, Mount.
Flint, Jr., George M.	see, Flints Point.
Fort Ross Colony	see, Kalifornsky.
Foster, Neal Winston	see, Foster, Mount.
Fritts, Dr. Crawford E.	see, Fritts Mountain.
Genet, Raymond Edward	see, Pirate Lake.
Gisel, Charles Alonzo	see, Gisel Peak.
Golub, Harvey	see, Golub, Mount.
Grant, U. S.	see, Northwestern Glacier.
Green, Joshua	see, Joshua Green Peak.
Gruening, Ernest	see, Ernest Gruening, Mount.
Guilbeau, Samuel	see, Guilbeau Pass.
Hankinson, Cmdr. Ray L.	see, Hankinson Peninsula.
Hanus, Cmdr. Gustavus Charles	see, Hanus Islet.
Harding Ice Field	see, Exit Glacier.
Herning, Orville George	see, Herning Lake.
Hislop, John	see, Hislop, Mount.
Holen, Chelle	see, Chelle Lake.
Holen, Lee	see, Chelle Lake.
Imperial Russian Navy	see, Fankuda Islet; Sealion Rocks.
International Geological Congress	see, McLeod, Point.
International Sourdoughs	see, Lulu Fairbanks, Mount.
Inualurak, Hugo	see, Inualurak Mountain.
Izmaylov, G. A.	see, Bocharov Island; Izmaylov Island.
Johnson, Harold A.	see, Johnson Rock.
Johnson, Robert R.	see, Bob Johnson Lake.
Jonas, Florence	see, Kalhabuk Mountain.
Jones, Roy Franklin	see, Roy Jones Mountain.
Kalmbach, George F.	see, Kalmbach Lake.
Karluk (vessel)	see, Bartlett Island.
Knopf, Adolph	see, Adolph Knopf, Mount.
Korn, Robert Wade	see, Robert Korn, Mount.
Kramer, Clarence E.	see, Clarence Kramer Peak.
Krause, Arthur	see, Krause, Mount.
Krause, Aurel	see, Krause, Mount.
Langille, William Alexander	see, Langille Mountain.
Ledyard, John	see, Ledyard Bay.
Leffingwell, Ernest de Koven	see, Leffingwell Fork.
Leland, O. M.	see, Leland, Mount.
Loberg, Lauritz Konrad Moller	see, Loberg Lake.
Lohi, August	see, Lohi Creek.
London, Jack	see, London, Mount.
Loon (vessel)	see, Loon Shoal.

Lowell, Capt. Frank   see, Alice, Mount.
Lutke, Capt. F. P.   see, Sealion Rocks.

McLeod, Bruce Berns   see, McLeod Lake.
Mandy, Mildred, V.   see, Manty Mountain.
Maptigak, Morry   see, Maptigak Mountain.
Martin, Lawrence   see, Rasmusson Glacier; Rasmusson, Mount.
Matanuska (vessel)   see, Johnson Rock.
Mitchell, Brig. Gen. William   see, Billy Mitchell, Mount.
Molver, John Ragnvard   see, Molver Island.
Moore, Cmdr. Edwin King.   see, Haley Rocks.
Moore, Lt. William   see, Captain William Moore Creek;
                                                            Reynard Point.

Nichols, Lt. Comdr. H. E.   see, Breezy Bay.
Northwest Trading Company   see, Dickinson Glacier.
Northwestern University   see, Northwestern Glacier.

Oglala (vessel)   see, Saint Markarius Point.

Palfy, Paul   see, Paul, Lake.
Payne, Judge   see, Payne Island.
Perue, Norman   see, Perue Peak.
Princess Maquinna (vessel)   see, McLeod, Point.
Project Snow Cornice   see, Foresta, Mount.
Pullen, Harriet   see, Pullen, Mount.

Raatikainen, Kalle   see, Raatikainen, Mount.
Rasmusson, E. A.   see, Rasmusson Glacier; Rasmusson, Mount.
Ray, L.V.   see, L V Ray Peak.
Rhode, Cecil   see, Cecil Rhode Mountain.
Rock, Howard   see, Weyahok River.
Rokita, Emil   see, Emil Lake.

Sarichev, Lt. G. A.   see, Fankuda Islet.
Sasby, John   see, Sasby Island.
Scheffler, Alice Lowell   see, Alice, Mount.
Service, Robert   see, Service, Mount.
Sheldon, Don E.   see, Don Sheldon Amphitheater.
Shiels, Archibald Williamson   see, Shiels, Mount.
Solf, John D.   see, Solf Lake.
Spencer, Arthur Coe   see, Spencer Peak.
Stefansson, Dr. Vilhjalmar   see, Stefansson Sound.
Stefansson Expedition   see, Bartlett Island.
Stevens, Sen. Ted   see, Begich Peak; Boggs Peak.
Stewart, Benjamin D.   see, Ben Stewart, Mount.
Sullivan, John H.   see, Sullivan Creek.
Swedish Evangelical Mission Covenant of America   see, Rasmusson Glacier; Rasmusson, Mount.
Symonds, Lt. F. M.   see, Hanus Islet.

Tarr, Ralph S.	see, Rasmusson Glacier; Rasmusson, Mount.
Taylor, A. Wayne	see, Wayne Taylor Peak.
Tebenkov, M. D.	see, Polovina Point.
Thibodeaux, Jules	see, Thibodeaux Mountain.
Three Saints (vessel)	see, Bocharov Island, Izmaylov Island.
Tobin, Emery F.	see, Emery Tobin, Lake.
Tundra Times	see, Weyahok River.
Tyndall, John	see, Tyndall Glacier.

U. S. Air Force	see, Balchen, Mount.
U. S. Atomic Energy Commission	see, C. P. Bluff.
U. S. Bureau of Land Management	see, Cravens Peak.
U. S. Chugach National Forest	see, Langille Mountain.
U. S. Coast and Geodetic Survey	see, Westdahl Point.
U. S. Coast Guard	see, Bittersweet Rock.
U. S. Coast Survey	see, Reynarad, Point.
U. S. Congress	see, Bartlett Hills; Begich Peak; Boggs Peak; Ernest Gruening, Mount.
U. S. Geological Survey	see, Adolph Knopf, Mount; Blankenship Creek; Boulder Patch; Chapin Peak; Flints Point.
U. S. Kenai National Moose Range	see, Big Merganser Lake; Langille Mountain; Little Merganser Lake.
U. S. National Oceanic and Atmospheric Admin.	see, Davidson Bay; Rainier Island.
U. S. Navy	see, Breezy Bay; Haley Rocks; Hanus Islet; Reynard, Point.
U. S. Office of Air Service	see, Bob Johnson Lake.
U. S. Old Kasaan National Monument	see, Langille Mountain.
U. S. Sitka National Monument	see, Langille Mountain.

Vasiliev, Ivan	see, Fankuda Islet.

Ward, Jonathan F.	see, Jonathan Ward, Mount.
Wakefield, Lee Howard	see, Port Wakefield.
Wakefield, Lowell A.	see, Lowell Wakefield, Mount.
Wakefield Fisheries	see, Lowell Wakefield, Mount.
Walatka, John	see, Walatka Mountains.
Warbelow, Marvin E.	see, Warbelow, Mount.
Waugh, Harold (Hal)	see, Hal Waugh, Mount.
White Pass and Yukon Railroad	see, Hislop, Mount.
Witsoe, Hank	see, Witsoe Lake.
Wood, Foresta H.	see, Foresta, Mount.
Woolfe, Henry D.	see, Woolfe Fork.
Wrather, William Embry	see, Wrather, Mount.

Zagoskin, Lt. Laurenti Alexief	see, Zagoskin Lake.